D1625315

The Satirist's Art

THE
Satirist's Art

EDITED BY

H. JAMES

Jensen

&

MALVIN R.

Zirker, Jr.

Bloomington

INDIANA UNIVERSITY PRESS

London

PR 935
S26
1972

827.09
S 253

Copyright © 1972 by Indiana University Press
All rights reserved
No part of this book may be reproduced or utilized in any form
or by any means, electronic or mechanical, including photocopying
and recording, or by any information storage and retrieval system,
without permission in writing from the publisher. The Association
of American University Presses Resolution on Permissions constitutes
the only exception to this prohibition.
Published in Canada by Fitzhenry & Whiteside Limited,
Don Mills, Ontario
Library of Congress catalog card number: 79–182268
ISBN: 0–253–35080–8
Manufactured in the United States of America

Contents

AUG 2 8 1972

Preface

The following papers by Earl Miner, Michael Rosenblum, and Ernest Tuveson were given under pleasant circumstances in Bloomington, Indiana, March 16 and 17, 1970, at the sixth Indiana University Eighteenth Century Conference. The conference was a part of the Indiana University Sesquicentennial Celebration, and we thank the Sesquicentennial Committee and the Indiana University Foundation for their very generous support. The papers appear in the same order and essentially as given at the conference. The Introduction and Afterword were contributed by the editors.

H.J.J.
M.R.Z.

Introduction

H. James Jensen

Satire has always provoked discussion. It is exciting and pertinent, and has been so ever since people began calling each other
names and criticizing each other's actions. But from the beginning of recorded opinion up to the present time, what has been
written has described satire, whether as mode or as genre, and
this leads us to a second, more scholarly attraction. Despite all
that has been written, no one has defined satire's essence. It is not
surprising, therefore, that the three excellent papers given at the
1970 Indiana University Eighteenth Century Conference are
three forceful attempts to explain the problem of what satire (or
a satire) is and how it works. Their authors, Messrs. Miner,
Rosenblum, and Tuveson, assume the difficult task of getting at
essentials, and they all agree (as do most of their predecessors)
that what is essential to satire, and certainly to eighteenth-century
satire, is rhetorical in nature. Although I balk at using so general
a term as rhetorical, no other will do because no other that I can
think of means precisely the art of arranging words and ideas to
produce certain, planned effects in an audience.

Satire's essence is as illusive as the center of Peer Gynt's onion.
It is unlike other important kinds of literature because it lacks a

definable cathartic effect, or at least so far, no one has isolated a general effect closely enough for generic definition. By cathartic effect, I mean the combination of a person's physical and emotional response to a work of art. The physical and emotional effects that different tragedies produce, for example, are, as Aristotle recognized, in most cases somewhat similar, and although Aristotle's definition of tragedy has been stretched to include varieties other than those he knew, the cathartic effect is still tragedy's essence. Satire, however, forces us to consider broader questions of rhetoric: descriptions of style, and analyses of authors' intentions. The lack of cathartic effect does not particularly bother us when we talk about or describe formal verse satire, which is pretty much limited by Roman models, and can often be described as secular sermons. But what we usually call the great English satires are not formal verse satires. They are not secular sermons, although they may be "exempla" of sermons. The eighteenth century in England produced more than its share of these odd works, and the main characteristics of the great eighteenth-century English satires are general enough: they tell stories, or versions of history; their writers or personae or voices assume the appropriate (often ironic) ethos or moral stance; and they usually have to do with abuses, excrescences, or stupidities imagined or found in the world of day-to-day existence. *Absalom and Achitophel, MacFlecknoe, The Dunciad, The Rape of the Lock,* and *Gulliver's Travels,* in varying degrees, are all of this nature, and it is with these and other eighteenth-century satires as background that the excellent papers in this volume come to grips with their slippery subject.

Although each paper deals with a different work, or works, and although each varies from the others in approach, all assume correctly that the authors under consideration are self-consciously rhetorical. Earl Miner, whose paper is more theoretical than the others, and can, therefore, be used as a point of departure, talks of what he calls "transformation." The first assumption he makes in developing his concept is the idea that a satirist had a conscious or deliberate intent. The problem of intention is rhetorical. We start to see the poet as persuader, as inventor, and as craftsman, a "maker" of art (imaginatively designed and conceived artifacts). The two other authors, also, make the assumption of intent before they sally forth, each in a different direction, Michael Rosenblum to Pope's *Dunciad* and Ernest Tuveson to Swift's fierce indignation. Mr. Rosenblum says that satire is "self-conscious," and Mr. Tuveson says we "comprehend rightly Swift's greatness" by examining the "ends and means" of his art. Both lead us to believe that works like *The Dunciad* or *Gulliver's Travels* are certainly highly contrived and finely wrought.

Miner further develops the idea of "transformation" by explaining how "the poet transforms all that relevantly exists in him and about him as he creates," and he uses the emblem of the "falling city" to describe the satirist's view of reality, an emblem which is the reverse of panegyrics devoted to cities' greatnesses. He argues convincingly that "panegyric" and "satiric" are opposite, extreme views of reality which depend on each other for their effective existence. This can be illustrated by testimonies of artists who note that neoplatonic visions of heavenly beauty and perfection occur simultaneously with visions of ugliness and chaos.[1] When Miner says that the mode of satire is degeneration, whereas that of panegyric is apotheosis, he is defining a natural genre, not based on a theory of catharsis but on the poet's vision of reality. His definition is rather general, but it is hard to deny, and is at least a good start. It appears to be a twentieth-century version of a traditional, pragmatic, rhetorical analysis of composition, based on art as a probable imitation of nature. The traditional version includes relative points of view: you can see something as better (panegyrical view) or worse (satirical view) than it sometimes might appear. The conception of art as imitating nature, improving on or debasing it, gives latitude to artists and poets and subsumes a natural theory of genres, of which, of course, satire is one. Miner then unites the rhetorical considerations of author, work of art, and audience, saying that the "fearsome powers" that satire possesses act on an audience very much according to the perceived intention of the author. The implication is that the author can control the audience to a more or less effective degree.

From these theoretical speculations, we can move logically in two directions: the first is to a satire as a self-contained work of art, the poet's vision of reality unrelated to or unconcerned with the world; the second to the idea that satire causes things to happen, that its importance is in its persuasive effects on readers. The first direction is the way taken by Rosenblum. His paper concerns primarily the idea envisioned by the poet, in this case Pope, as his poetic vision becomes through rhetoric an artistic monument (called *The Dunciad*). To refute the idea that satire has to cause things to happen, Mr. Rosenblum very wittily points out that reality, sometimes at least, seems to imitate Pope's art, rather than vice versa. He also chooses to see Pope's rhetoric as ornamental, giving us an imaginative vision, or "version" of history, which may or may not have anything to do with worldly existence. Lord Hervey of history becomes, therefore, unimportant; his significance is only in Pope's book: "Pope and the reader are not interested in who the dunce is, but only in what can be made of him. This seems to me the general issue of *The Dunciad*: how may the deeds of dullness be converted into an act of wit?" *The Dunciad* is primarily a work of art, an artifact, something separate from the world.

Rosenblum shows us the importance of a rhetorical definition of satire in his comments on the final lines of *The Dunciad*. He says that Pope is in danger of losing us in his destructive vision, that he may go too far to restore "the common forms of wit, order, and civilization" as exempt from the satirist's negative vision. Rosenblum's theoretical reasoning is similar to the view that satire projects "a dark view of reality." But he is criticizing a specific work. And he does so in generic terms, tentatively saying that the dialectic between panegyric poetry and satire is lost, that the destructive vision obscures the positive vision so much that the effect (as generally as we have seen that effect defined) is distorted beyond satire's realm. In other words, Pope's artistic monument may crush the audience's imagination rather than capture it, and the effect of annihilation emanates directly from the artistic vision and its execution. Perhaps Pope has overstepped the bounds of satire as a particular view of reality. Rosenblum's last point, that satire need not cause something to happen in the real world, indicates that the poet's vision of reality, not a cathartic effect, is most important in defining the relative success of Pope's conclusion.

The second direction concerns effect. Satires often make us "feel" something: that sinking feeling we have when a poet points out to us that the world is not what we would wish it to be, such as Samuel Pepys's reaction to Marvell's "Last Instructions to the Painter" or our own reactions to the ubiquitous satirical accounts of the state of mankind. If satire is to reform and improve the world, then it should chasten and change, for as Tuveson says, such is the professed intention of most satiric writers. If there is no individual change, satire has no real effect. Unfortunately, we almost always think that satire applies to someone else. Tuveson believes that Swift alone, in *Gulliver's Travels,* has made the world feel satire's lash, showing us the futility of a definition of satire which is cathartic rather than rhetorical in origin. He does not use *Gulliver's Travels* as a documentary of Swift's neuroses or as evidence of his decayed mind. He analyzes Swift's rhetoric, his intentions in his satire, and the success with which he carried them out, noting that Swift's ability to control his audience is exactly what makes him so great. After a soundly and powerfully argued essay, his conclusion is simple and profound: "Swift's importance is narrow but deep; it lies in his mastery of his particular kind of art, of its technique in relation to his intentions, not in the special complexity and originality of his insight into the depths of human nature; and so it is by examining that art, its ends and means, that we come to comprehend rightly Swift's greatness."

Both Tuveson's and Rosenblum's approach are practical demonstrations of the implications of Miner's image of "transformation." All three see satire bounded by an essentially rhetorical nature, a nature generically defined by the author's vision of reality and his art, rather than by the assumed uniformity of effect satire has on its audience. But the unity I have tried to explain is only a view from outside the essays, as well as outside satire. I do injustice to the essays to stop here, and Malvin Zirker raises many more issues expressed in them in his Afterword. Suffice it to say that all four essays offer fresh, intelligent views of their subjects, substantial scholarly contributions to the study of satire, enjoyable reading, and for those who attended the Indiana University Eighteenth Century Conference, a reminder of a very pleasant, congenial time.

The Satirist's Art

In
Satire's Falling City

Earl Miner
UNIVERSITY OF CALIFORNIA, LOS ANGELES

urbs antiqua ruit, multos dominata per annos.
Virgil, *Aeneid*
All humane things are subject to decay.
Dryden, *MacFlecknoe*

The import of my title will be plain to anyone who recalls
Juvenal's third satire, in which Rome at night knows no repose,
and its citizens encounter hordes of their fellows, the dangers of
houses crashing in flames, brickbats or chamberpots thrown into
the street, or a casual beam swinging towards one's head. But
the phrase also parodies an English Christmas carol that I had
once thought to use for an epigraph to a chapter on *Absalom
and Achitophel*: "Once in David's royal city." In choosing the
collapsing city as an emblem, I forfeit the opportunity to use
certain others, and may seem to omit from consideration a number of important works. The complaints of the medieval Plow-
man, or the beast fables of Spenser's *Mother Hubbards Tale*

and of Gulliver's fourth voyage, may well spring to mind. But an emblem seeks a wider truth through limited representation, and at the least it will be recognized that the satire of the Restoration and the eighteenth century is, like Donne's and Juvenal's, normally located in an urban scene.

More than that, the city has long been a symbol of the state and of civilization. Rome gave its name to an empire as well as to a way of life, and its citizens dated years from the foundation of the city. For all the changes brought by time, Athens means democracy and an idea held by Plato in his *Republic*. Rome came to mean empire, and Venice a republic. The philosophical and literary significance implied by the city has been recognized by acute modern observers,[1] and to Hobbes it represented for literature, comedy in its dramatic version, satire in its narrative.[2] From Baudelaire, Eliot took for his *Waste Land* the symbol of the "Unreal City" for dessicated modern life. Horace has long proved, in what I may risk calling his urbane way, the most obstinate of major satiric poets to those of us who venture to theorize about the genre. Yet his "Town Mouse and Country Mouse" (II, vi) confirm my emblem, and so, I believe, do such seeming exceptions as the "Journey to Brundisium" (I, v) in which the first two lines are built on a contrast between "grand Rome" and the "modest inn," or Aricia, the significance of which contrast was fully recognized by such editors as those of the Delphin Horace.[3] Until its end, the journey presents degenerate versions of the city left behind. Just as much that lies deep within human experience and much that is sanctioned by literary tradition has led to depiction of country life as the *vita beata,* so have equally powerful forces led centuries of writers to identify the city with civilization, and the deterioration of the city with the satirist's art.

Something more than convenience compels us, then, to the belief that we may represent the central concern of satire in the process of the ruin of an ideal city. The fall of "fair *Augusta* much to fears inclin'd" is related in that passage of *MacFlecknoe* to the ruined tower of Barbican (64–73); and on its ruins, as on the London of *The Dunciad,* a lasting night falls. The polar opposite of this process is the raising by panegyric of "the enduring monument," the conferring of an immortality immune to time the devourer of things, as Ovid suggests.[4] The symbol of the city exists in other, non-satiric versions. Aeneas, who has fled burning Troy and who is on his way to establish Rome, exclaims over monumental Carthage, "O fortunate they, whose walls already rise." [5] The taking of an enemy city is of course also an epic subject, as the *Iliad* and *Gerusalemme Liberata* well show. And a movement altogether contrary to the satiric version will be found in that from the earthly to the heavenly Jerusalem in biblical prophecy and exegesis, or from Augustine's Rome to his City of God. In satire, we are within the gates, and so is the enemy. We have only the faintest or the most implied of memories of the firm goodness that was, and the strongest sense of stone, burning timbers, and refuse cascading down. Satire depicts, then, in this emblem, a process of ruin. Dryden might choose for his epigraph to *Annus Mirabilis* a line from the *Aeneid* (II, 363), "An ancient and imperial city falls," but he depicts at the close of the poem a transformed city rising from the ashes:

> More great then humane, now, and more *August,*
> New deifi'd she from her fires does rise:
> Her widening streets on new foundations trust,
> And, opening, into larger parts she flies. (1177–1180)

There is no such rise to be seen in *MacFlecknoe* or *The Dunciad.*

Enough for now of emblems. The truth is that we know very little about the real principles animating the major literary kinds.

No modern definition of tragedy with which I am acquainted takes into account all three plays of the only surviving Greek trilogy, the *Oresteia*. I confess to having cracked my own teeth on such smaller nuts as the fable and the verse epistle. Of course if we use such Latin terms as *epistula* or *metrica epistola,* it sounds as if we have come on a Lamarckian vocabulary. But I fancy that we have done more for our self-esteem than our understanding. And yet satire can lay claim to being one of the best understood of the major genres of Western literature. We have had a number of recent studies of the formal properties and attributes of verse satire in particular, of satiric fictions, examinations of satiric *topoi* and process, and of course numerous revealing discussions of individual satiric works.[6] Not only that. We can turn to such humanists as J. C. Scaliger, Daniel Heinsius, or Causabon for lengthy (if rather turgid) treatises, and to Dryden, whose longest prose essay on a single genre more or less stays with this subject.[7] We have, then, histories of satiric writing, theories as to its forms, and discussions of individual satires. And if we have any sense, we must say that for such mercies we give thanks.

In counting our blessings, I have not been able to say that theory and analysis often go together. I doubt that such major verse satires as *MacFlecknoe, The Medall, The Rape of the Lock,* and *The Dunciad* have much benefited from discussions of the "formal verse satire." And if there has been published any meaningful discussion of that essence shared by Donne's second satire, the second voyage of *Gulliver's Travels,* and the second act of *The Beggars' Opera,* I confess my ignorance of it. It is with some confidence that I can promise that my discussion will not leave other students of this protean form so many Othellos, their occupation gone. All that I can hope to do is to begin with a premise about the nature of literary process, develop a description of the workings of satire in ways moving from the simple to the complex, and then hope to fly the falling city of satire before I am found out.

My premise about literature eschews numerous theories, including the mimetic. My inclination to this heresy is not so strong as to lead me, like Luther, to nail my theses on the door of the Augustan temple. When I return to my premise later it will be found mild enough, and at this stage I may simply say that I believe literature to be a process, not of imitation or of organic growth or of formalism, but of a dual transformation. The Poet transforms all that relevantly exists in him and about him as he creates, and the Reader transforms all that he musters in him and in his process of reading the Poem.[8] The transformational hypothesis merely assumes that the Poet acts, as it were, inclusively in his process of making the Poem, and the Reader as it were exclusively in transforming the poem afresh, personally, in remaking the Poem in his own reading. In what ensues, various Poets' transformations as understood and indeed transformed by one Reader will be the subject of discussion. And by putting a mild heresy so simply I shall have begged enough questions not to be charged with anything worse than platitude. I take it, then, that I am safe. To resume my heresy and shortly to return to satire, I shall say that artistic transformation presumes a deliberate act, if not that dread thing, intention. When life imitates art, our response may resemble that to art, but the differences are essential. As one addicted to book catalogues, I came upon the following not long ago.

> POTATOES: Production, Storing, Processing. By Ora Smith, Ph.D., in collaboration with a group of specialists. . . . In this, the first comprehensive book on the subject, Dr. Ora Smith has condensed the results of a lifetime of study devoted principally to the potato, and has provided a summary of a cross section of the latest results of research by many investigators in the field throughout the world.[9]

The whole point of our amusement resides in the inadvertent, undeliberate nature of this nonsense. There is no felt intelligence in operation, and none of the deliberate focus that is required for satire or any transforming art. By contrast, we detect a very different, more deliberate, hand in the following skit from *gesta satirae* from a recent issue of *The Scriblerian*: "A new Pope scholar, John Richard Clark, from Twitnam Gardens, New York, has announced his forthcoming book: *Feathered Synolon: Bird Imagery as a Unity Factor in a Reading of Pope's Letters*." [10] We believe that Dr. Smith has indeed written about the study of the potato in the field, and we assent with a different faith when the editors of *The Scriblerian* transform a lamentable scholarly tendency into satiric art.

Such an act of deliberation in satiric art inevitably implied rhetoric to seventeenth- and eighteenth-century writers. As the anonymous author of *Raillerie à la Mode Considered* put it in 1673, bantering writers possess "a Sort of Natural Rhetorick." The armory of the satirists' natural devices is set forth as "their Dry Bobs, their Broad Flouts, Bitter Taunts, their Fleering Frumps, and Privy Nips." [11] How very natural a "Rhetorick," we say, for Restoration banter and satire. Yet in fact these delightful phrases come straight out of Puttenham, who coined them as English equivalents for classical rhetorical terms.[12] The "Natural Rhetorick" of satire turns out to be our costive old friend, the *Ars Rhetoricae,* memorized by, or whipped into, schoolboys in former centuries. The boldfaced appropriation of Puttenham by our anonymous writer reveals not only the tendency for the arms of the rhetorician to show through the ragged sleeves of the satirist, but also for satire to imitate the shapes and forms of non-satiric writers. Such appropriation scarcely requires much illustration, but let me emphasize my belief that the process entails transformation rather than simple parody. In *MacFlecknoe* Dryden is unusual in shaping panegyric into its rhetorical opposite, satire, but the poem is not strictly a mock-encomium like Erasmus' *Praise of Folly.* Nor is it true in any important sense that there is parody in such imitations as Pope's of Horace in *To Augustus* or Dr. Johnson's of Juvenal in *The Vanity of Human Wishes.*

Another element that must accompany such appropriation in order for transformation to be possible is a fresh momentum, a new energy. This can be seen in a minor example, a limiting case. Early in the Restoration it was natural that somebody should seize on the almanac as a form to alter into satire. It was natural, because of the extraordinary popularity of the form, and because predictions by William Lilly and others had flourished so intensely during the Commonwealth and Protectorate. *Montelions Almanack: For 1661* (London, 1661) is a gay-hearted version of what Butler's sardonically observed Sidrophel might have published. In it, there is much that tastes of the bitter portion of satiric transformation, but we also find in it that humor, that pure inventive whimsy, which takes what might be only a parody into the realm of independent satiric vitality. The following prediction will be found in *"Octobers* Observations":

> This month a *phenix* shall come into *England* and build her a nest of sweetwood in Hide-park, and all the Citizens Wives shall go forth to see her, after this she shall fly away and sit upon the top of *Salisbury Spire* three days and three nights together. Then shall the Universities flourish so that there shall not be found above one dunce in a Colledge. (sig. C3ʳ)

It is the free energy that helps this little satiric phoenix take flight.

It is quite true that my browsing in book catalogues and in the ephemera shelved not so ephemerally in the Clark Library does little to advance theoretical understanding of the nature of satire. To take any larger step, we must turn to a major writer and critic such as Dryden. After rambling on a variety of interesting topics for above seventy pages, his *Discourse Concerning the Original and Progress of Satire* comes at last to the rules for "designing of a perfect satire." [13] The first is "that it ought only to treat of one subject; to be confined to one particular theme; or at least, to one principally." [14] His second rule "for perfecting the design of true satire" follows from the first: "The poet is bound, and that *ex officio,* to give his reader some one precept of moral virtue, and to caution him against some one particular vice or folly." [15] This rule clearly offers the moral or thematic counterpart of the structural first rule. A third, dealing with "the best and finest manner of satire," slips in almost unnoticed in a concern with satiric style. That is, raillery (not railing) is to be preferred, or at least a "sharp, well-mannered way of laughing a folly out of countenance." [16] Finally, there is "the most beautiful and most noble kind of satire," that with "the majesty of the heroic, finely mixed with the venom of the other." Such satire clearly requires "beautiful turns of words and thoughts; which are as requisite in this, as in heroic poetry itself, of which the satire is undoubtedly a species." [17]

All this tells us a great deal about Dryden's conception of what good satire should be, but it reveals surprisingly little about what satire is *per se.* Like many a critic, Dryden shifts much too quickly from description to normative demands. That is, although he begins descriptively, and indeed prescriptively, with rules for "designing" satiric poetry, he really concerns himself with the best kinds rather than with the genus proper. I am prepared to believe that satire written on his plan may indeed be the "noblest." But I cannot believe that satire need possess one subject, that it must advance just one moral cause, or that it must attack "one particular vice or folly." Certainly I cannot believe that it is necessary for satire to be written in a high style or to have any connection with epic. It is remarkable how Plato and Aristotle,

Horace and Boileau, and now Dryden turn from what may loosely be called descriptive to normative definitions. Not only that, criticism of the classical kind is remarkably given to prescription, and even the greatest critics seem to imply that what is not the best of its kind does not really belong to the kind at all. Yet Dryden is forced to admit that Horace and Samuel Butler fit but ill into his rules. And I doubt the utility of his norms for Donne, Rochester, Oldham, and most of Pope. One wonders how much might be salvaged from them for application to the prose satire by Swift.

Nonetheless, it remains true that what a major critic sets as his optimum may put us on the track to find out what he and we may think is essential. Surely the clue is in that arresting double phrase, "heroic poetry itself, of which the satire is undoubtedly a species." How odd that seems. On the other hand, many people have quoted, out of its context in a difficult poem, Dryden's remark that "Satire will have room, where e're I write." [18] In fact, it is the heroic that proves to be the more pervasive in his poetry and his critical thought: "The evidence from the beginning to the end is everywhere." [19]

Two very different implications emerge, one of them only indirectly and almost by accident, from this characteristic Drydenian assimilation. The first is that we must distinguish between works that are satires (or epics) and works that possess satiric (or heroic) elements in them but which are not radically satires (or epics). Surely the point about *The Rape of the Lock* is that it blends something of the heroic with something of the satiric in a new formulation also admitting the lyric and the panegyric. If we call the poem a satire, we mean, if we mean anything at all, that the satiric element predominates. If we call it a mock heroic, we mean that the satiric element is more wholly balanced by the epic. About one-fifth of *Absalom and Achitophel* is clearly satiric, part of it is panegyric, part of it epic, and part dis-

cursive. On the other hand, *MacFlecknoe, The Medall,* the
Fable of the Bees, and Pope's labeled satires are satires properly
speaking, because the radical satiric element stipulates the terms
on which such other elements as the lyric or the epic may be
admitted. To my mind, Pope is at his greatest when two radical
elements or attitudes are held in poise, as are satire and epic
throughout *The Rape of the Lock* or at the end of *The Dunciad.*
Other forms of poise raise to highest distinction the opening of
the second epistle of *The Essay on Man* and the epistle to
Bathurst, which is almost my favorite among his poems.

From my drifting away from my topic, it will be clear that
Dryden's power of digression is one of the few of his critical
faculties that he bestows on his editors, so that I must regret that
I cannot praise Pope as intelligently as Dryden would have.
There was supposed to be, however, a second important implication to Dryden's making satire a species of the epic.[20] To draw
that out, we must move to one of his earlier critical pieces. More
than a quarter of a century before his long preface to the *Satires,*
he had written on proper "descriptions or images" in the Account
he prefixed to *Annus Mirabilis.*

> Such descriptions or images, well wrought, which I promise
> not for mine, are, as I have said, the adequate delight of
> heroic poesy; for they beget admiration, which is its proper
> object; as the images of the burlesque, which is contrary to
> this, by the same reason beget laughter: for the one shows
> nature beautified, as in the picture of a fair woman, which
> we all admire; the other shows her deformed, as in that of
> a lazar, or of a fool with distorted face and antic gestures,
> at which we cannot forbear to laugh, because it is a devia-
> tion from nature. But though the same images serve equally
> for the epic poesy, and for the historic and panegyric, which
> are branches of it, yet a several sort of sculpture is to be
> used in them.[21]

My students know all too well that I think this a crucial passage for understanding Dryden.[22] It affords us surprise at first by pairing burlesque with "heroic poesy." The reason for the pairing emerges later in the statement that historical and panegyric poetry are branches of epic. Having written in 1667 that panegyric was a major species of the genus epic, Dryden could write consistently in 1693 that satire was also. The consistency resides in the rhetorical fact that panegyric and satire are complementary forms of amplification. Whether we consider the "Natural Rhetorick" of *Raillerie à la Mode Considered,* or whether we examine the employment of the usual *topoi* of praise (origin, ancestry, great acts, testimony from others, testimony from the speaker, etc.), we soon come to see that satire and panegyric invert each other along very similar rhetorical lines.

It would be difficult to stress enough the rhetorical relation of satire to panegyric. Some people would accept, I think, a view that satire may cleverly manipulate praise, and they might instance *MacFlecknoe.* But although they would admit Pope's *To Augustus* as an example of satire transposing panegyric, they would probably doubt the possibility of the reverse movement, of making panegyric out of the grounds of satire. For reasons that I shall give later, it does seem true to me that the *movement* from the panegyric, or the *falling* of the satiric city, is essential to satire. And it must also be confessed that we can think more readily of poems like *To Augustus* than of panegyrics shoplifting in the satiric mart. But how many successful panegyrics come to mind? Even so, the process or movement from satire to affirmation can be observed on occasion. *MacFlecknoe* and *To My Dear Friend Mr. Congreve* bear uncanny resemblances to each other in imagery, subject matter, and use of rhetorical places. There is even the same parental situation and tone. For a specific instance, let us begin with a passage from *Paradise Lost*:

> High on a Throne of Royal State, which far
> Outshone the wealth of *Ormus* and of *Ind,* . . .
> Satan exalted sat, by merit rais'd
> To that bad eminence. (II, 1–2, 5–6)

For that epic version there is of course a satiric version in *Mac-Flecknoe.*

> The hoary Prince in Majesty appear'd,
> High on a Throne of his own Labours rear'd. (106–107)

My point is that the satiric version is rendered panegyric in the *Congreve.*

> Yet this I Prophesy; Thou shalt be seen,
> (Tho' with some short Parenthesis between:)
> High on the Throne of Wit . . . (51–53)

At the beginning of the second book of *The Dunciad,* Pope put the "high on a Throne" motif back into satire. We whose school years did not entail the composing of exercises arguing on both sides of the question—whether day is better than night, riches than wisdom, age than youth, and so on—are far less receptive to the uses of the commonplaces and of the varieties of amplification possible in either direction of satire or of panegyric. But John Cleveland understood the fact perfectly and stated it plainly: "Libells are commendations, when revers'd." [23]

But, someone may be asking himself at this point, does not this talk about the rhetorical functioning of satire merely describe seventeenth- and eighteenth-century satire to the exclusion of other possibilities? The question is very fair, and to it I shall reply that there is a "Natural Rhetorick" of satire in the basic contrast with which I began, between the implicit, ideal city and the falling city of satire. Only the presumption of a good state enables us to call the present satiric one bad. And it is easy enough to show that the reverse is true in panegyric, as my earlier quotation of the epigraph and a late stanza from *Annus Mira-bilis* show. There the fallen city rises like a phoenix. The satiric city is very different in *MacFlecknoe*.

> Close to the Walls which fair *Augusta* bind,
> (The fair *Augusta* much to fears inclin'd)
> An ancient fabrick, rais'd t'inform the sight,
> There stood of yore, and *Barbican* it hight:
> A watch Tower once; but now, so Fate ordains,
> Of all the Pile an empty name remains. (64–69)

London, the city of Augustus, has not indeed totally fallen, but just that part of it belonging to those satirized. And how appropriate it is to a poem on the generically dull poet, one who never is quoted for a word in the poem, one whose single action is to sit, that his version of the poetic tower should be left only "an empty name." The architecture of dullness is not so much fallen as vanished. Dryden makes this clear by an echo a bit later (l. 82) from Davenant's *Gondibert*: MacFlecknoe will reign, precisely, "Amidst this Monument of vanisht minds." [24] We are all familiar with the darkness that uncreatingly descends at the end of *The Dunciad,* but most readers seem to have missed the ghostly quality of *MacFlecknoe*. MacFlecknoe is to rule over all the lands between barbarous Ireland and the barbaric Barbadoes, which is, as Dr. Johnson would have put it, an ideal vacancy. The crowd at his coronation consists of "the Nations," and yet, with few exceptions, they are all dead:

> But scatter'd Limbs of mangled Poets lay:
> From dusty shops neglected Authors come,
> Martyrs of Pies, and Reliques of the Bum. (99–101)

The apotheosis of MacFlecknoe will be a translation to "Some peacefull Province in Acrostick Land" (206). And Flecknoe himself is shortly thereafter translated down a stage trapdoor, reminding us that all has been a play as non-existent as the dramas

of Shadwell: "What share have we in Nature or in Art?" (176).
To the seventeenth century, that which shared neither in art nor
nature simply had no existence whatsoever. One part of the city
of Augustus has fallen into utter oblivion; the poetic tower has
crumbled and disappeared. So natural is this rhetoric of satire,
this contrast of the ideal city of Augustus with the ruin and loss,
that in constructing their ideal cities, utopian writers, as we have
learned recently, reflect upon the inferior city that actually exists.[25]
It is not true that utopias are simply satires, or satires failed
utopias, but by setting out extreme versions of each other, they
depend to some extent on each other's existence to keep them in
being. It is this kind of interplay between the two cities that is
the fundamental "Natural Rhetorick" of satire, and the particular
version of the natural in classical arts of rhetoric merely serves
to show that we have much to learn from older formulations
about literature.

I must now take a further step to complicate the discussion and
bring it closer to Dryden's discussion and, I believe, to what most
of us would regard as the truth of the matter. Between that
golden phoenix of London reborn in *Annus Mirabilis* and the
vanished tower in *MacFlecknoe,* as indeed between the cities
of satire and those of utopias, there exists the real city. Dryden is
at one with our earlier critics in terming that reality "nature," and
his theory is thoroughly mimetic: "The imitation of nature is
therefore justly constituted as the general, and indeed the only,
rule of pleasing, both in poetry and painting." [26] In the same
essay, the "Parallel of Poetry and Painting," Dryden offers us a
very revealing comment.

> In the character of an hero, as well as in an inferior figure,
> there is a better or worse likeness to be taken: the better is
> panegyric, if it be not false, and the worse is a libel.[27]

In other words, art takes a "likeness" of nature; and, we must
observe, it is wholly possible to take opposite kinds of likeness

and still remain with truth. As long as panegyric or satire take their likenesses in a way that is not "false," they retain their integrity.

At that I must enter a reservation. Unless I am mistaken, the bounds of truth are not the subject of an oath by a poet praising or satirizing. The important thing allowed by Dryden's theory is that there is felt to be a truth, a "nature," from which both panegyric and satire take their likenesses in order to achieve the ends of praise or blame.

Such ends are of course moral, evaluative. In making our own moral decisions and evaluations about literature, we tend to obscure the distinction between Dryden's "nature" and his "likeness." That is, the morality of a panegyrist like Claudian calling a man so virtuous, and the rest, or of a satirist like Oldham calling a man so vile and the rest—this morality depends on the truth of what they say, which can only be verified by evidence outside the poem. The poem itself establishes its own world, its own city, whose laws tell us who is good or who is bad, and it is on such terms that it makes up its morals and its values. I have put this pretty strongly, because in fact I believe in a more intimate association of art with life than do most contemporary critics. I cannot think it possible to write a great poem on Caligula as legislator or Hitler as anthropologist. But these examples, like my formulation, are extreme. Normally we accept the poem's moral world, whether that be the world of Donne's lovers awaking abed in the morning, whether it be Milton's universe, Pope's London, or Swift's Lilliput. When we have difficulty in knowing what that moral world is, or whether, in Dryden's phrase, "a better or worse likeness" is being taken, then the problems multiply. Some works have seemed to their contemporaries unclear or false in their values. Defoe's *Shortest Way with the Dissenters,* some of Chekhov's plays, and T. S. Eliot's *Waste Land* afford us examples. Other works seem not to have troubled contemporaries

so much but baffle us. I confess to confusion over many aspects of
Hudibras, and although I usually confine my attention to the
seventeenth century, I understand that some disagreement exists
over the fourth voyage of *Gulliver's Travels.* We need to be
reasonably sure that "a better or worse likeness" is being taken.
The taking of a worse likeness, the process of the city's falling
in the artistic process of satire, must now be my concern. To this
point I have accepted as far as possible the mimetic view of art,
and where it seemed to me limited, I have tried to adapt it to fit
acceptable terms. At the same time, I confess that I have been
selective in quoting from Dryden's criticism, in order that I might
stress that literature, including satire, is a transforming rather
than a mimetic process.[28] A transformational view of literature
allows us to retain the very valuable insight given us by mimetic
theory into the relation of nature and art, as the seventeenth century never tired of putting it. While allowing us that, it still
emphasizes the process of creation. One of the deficiencies of the
mimetic theory is its omission of the reader. The reader (or
hearer) necessarily makes his own transformation of the likenesses taken, deciding whether the Houyhnhnms are fully meant
as a value for him, or only partly so, or not at all. In the re-
mainder of this discussion, however, I propose to absorb the
reader's transformation and that of the poet into a discussion of
the direction and power of satiric transformation.

A transformational theory presumes, I believe, that differing
kinds of literary experience, call them genres or whatever, have
differing modes of transformation. I feel no compunction in taking from Northrop Frye a conception of the comic mode as a
sequence by which a disordered world is reintegrated.[29] Tragedy,
I feel, provides us with a sequence in which a disastrous world
is integrated. The mode of panegyric is that of apotheosis, of
rendering immortal. And the mode of satire, like the vision of
satire, is one of degeneration.[30] What is, in Robert C. Elliott's

fine phrase, "the power of satire," is precisely a vision of man, the state, arts, or the world degenerating before one's eyes. Usually the process of degeneration involves a tendency throughout the satire to belittle in the literal sense. Even Dryden, who aims so characteristically at magnification, uses diminution in *The Medall,* substituting the part for the whole, and similar rhetorical devices. Another such device is the substitution of a paltry thing for a grand person or even, as Swift so brilliantly shows in *A Tale of a Tub,* for a whole system of thought and value. A common form of degeneration depicted is disease, and of course the satirist is the harsh physician for the severe malady.[31] Another form of degeneration will be found in parody, burlesque, and travesty. One of the most effective modes has been the altering of the image of man, and again Swift provides us, in *Gulliver's Travels,* with most remarkable examples. A common altering of man's image is his metamorphosis into a beast. Spenser's *Mother Hubbards Tale* is an early English example. Any of these techniques may be systematic and so produce something approaching allegory. It is remarkable that during the decades from the Restoration to about 1730 satire and allegory alike flourished, not necessarily together, but I think fruitfully for the spirit of the age. For if satires often employed something like allegory, surely the Vanity Fair scene in *The Pilgrim's Progress* employs something like satire. Some of the most interesting satires are interesting especially for their powers of integration in local passages by means of imagery (e.g., the beast comparison) that might otherwise be schematic. There is, for example, that extraordinarily powerful passage in Pope's *Epilogue to the Satires. Written in 1738. Dialogue II.* All readers of Pope will recall the "filthy Simile," as the Friend calls it, on the court wits feeding off each other from an original acorn of sense.

> Let Courtly Wits to Wits afford supply,
> As Hog to Hog in Huts of *Westphaly*;

If one, thro' Nature's Bounty or his Lord's,
Has what the frugal, dirty soil affords,
From him the next receives it, thick or thin,
As pure a Mess almost as it came in;
The blessed Benefit, not there confin'd,
Drops to the third who nuzzles close behind;
From tail to mouth, they feed, and they carouse;
The last, full fairly gives it to the House. (171–180)

Although a sustained conceit, this extraordinary simile is not systematic through the whole poem. What it does show is indeed "the power of satire."

I wish to dwell upon such power, or at least to illustrate it further, in order that I may make clear how profound a transformation satire entails. One may recall Gulliver's encounter with the monkey in Brobdingnag.

I have good reason to believe that he took me for a young one of his own species, by his often stroking my face very gently with his other paw. In these diversions he was interrupted by a noise at the closet door, as if somebody were opening it; whereupon he suddenly leaped up to the window at which he had come in, and thence upon the leads and gutters, walking upon three legs, and holding me in the fourth, till he clambered up to a roof that was next to ours. I heard Glumdalclitch give a shriek at the moment he was carrying me out. The poor girl was almost distracted: that quarter of the palace was all in an uproar; the servants ran for ladders; the monkey was seen by hundreds in the court, sitting upon the ridge of a building, holding me like a baby in one of his fore-paws, and feeding me with the other, by cramming into my mouth some victuals he had squeezed out of the bag on one side of his chaps, and patting me when I would not eat; whereat many of the rabble below could not forbear laughing; neither do I think they justly ought to be blamed, for without question the sight was ridiculous enough to every body but myself.[32]

Some very remarkable things happen in this passage. Man becomes a kind of beast, at least to a beast, and not without Swiftian point. Moreover, one of the surest experiences of security known to psychiatrists, the child's being fed by its mother, is here turned into a passage of surpassing danger and disgust. There is also the danger of fall from the heights in that nightmare world. But more remarkable than all else is the fact that Gulliver does not say a word, during his description, of *his own* response, whether of disgust, fear, or indeed of any reaction. The other actors react: "The poor girl was almost distracted." He is acted upon almost in entire passivity. Such an abstention from reaction in the course of that extraordinary degeneration forces the reader to make his own transformation, to supply his own emotional responses. And when he does, he does not arrive where Gulliver does. Gulliver's remark that it really was quite a funny sight is surely just about the last blow to our sense of equanimity.

Another powerful degenerative process employed by satire is the depiction of lust, and of all the many satiric versions, surely the most effective is Juvenal's depiction of Empress Messalina stealing from the side of Claudius as soon as he falls asleep.

> The good old Sluggard but began to snore,
> When from his side up rose th' Imperial Whore:
> She who preferr'd the Pleasures of the Night
> To Pomps, that are but impotent delight,
> Strode from the Palace, with an eager pace,
> To cope with a more Masculine Embrace:
> Muffl'd she march'd, like *Juno* in a Clowd,
> Of all her Train but one poor Wench allow'd,
> One whom in Secret Service she cou'd trust;
> The Rival and Companion of her Lust.

> To the known Brothel-house she takes her way; ⎱
> And for a nasty Room gives double pay;   ⎬
> That Room in which the rankest Harlot lay.   ⎰
> Prepar'd for fight, expectingly she lies,
> With heaving Breasts, and with desiring Eyes:
> Still as one drops, another takes his place,
> And baffled still succeeds to like disgrace.
> At length, when friendly darkness is expir'd,
> And every Strumpet from her Cell retir'd,
> She lags behind, and lingring at the Gate,
> With a repining Sigh, submits to Fate:
> All Filth without and all a Fire within,
> Tir'd with the Toyl, unsated with the Sin.
> Old *Caesar's* Bed the modest Matron seeks;
> The steam of Lamps still hanging on her Cheeks
> In Ropy Smut; thus foul, and thus bedight,
> She brings him back the Product of the Night.
> (VI, 163–189; trans. Dryden)

Lust is a token of degradation, but to an age conscious of social rank and filled with belief in the decencies of ceremony and the aura of regal divine right—indeed, even to us—the degeneration of an empress to a harlot is what gives the passage its ferocity.

Satire has of course many tones, and Horace for one is milder, more urbane. Dryden preferred Juvenal, at least on balance, and the fault he found with Horace the satirist was precisely his lack of force.

> Where he barely grins himself and, as Scaliger says, only shews his white teeth, he cannot provoke me to any laughter. His urbanity, that is, his good manners, are to be commended, but his wit is faint; and his salt, if I may dare to say so, almost insipid.[33]

Dryden's preference seems to be an English one. It is remarkable that when Donne adopted Horace's account of being accosted by an unremitting bore (*Satires,* I, 9), he turned it into a grave danger of being taken in by a court informer (*Satyre* IV). And even of that airiest of poems, *The Rape of the Lock,* Murray Krieger seems to me to have got at something essential with the title of his essay: "The 'Frail China Jar' and the Rude Hand of Chaos." [34] At all events, I am at one with Robert Elliott in thinking that in this milder age, in which we no longer laugh so easily at the grotesque nature of individuals, it is "the power of satire" that needs to be borne upon us. To that end, the version of satiric degenerative force that I wish finally to emphasize is the most fearsome of all, that leading to death.

It will be recalled that various collections of Royalist ballads and other verse were published together as *Rump Songs* in 1662, of course alluding, and often coarsely, to the Rump Parliament and the pertinent part of the body. What is less known is that in 1660 a shorter collection, subsequently incorporated into the *Rump Songs,* appeared under the title, *Ratts Rhimed to Death.* Here is the primitive basis of satire: you call your enemies rats, which is one kind of degeneration, and then you rhyme them to death, the last degeneration. That this was no passing fancy can be judged by a little volume of anti-Catholic poems published in 1683: *Rome Rhym'd to Death.* In his *Poetices* (VI, vii), J.C. Scaliger very well distinguishes between the lighter satiric effects common in the epistle after the manner of Horace and the far stronger measures of satire: "As verse epistles propound that by which we may avoid vice, satire goes to battle with those means by which vice can be extirpated." [35] One form propounds, the other fights a war to the death.

As Dryden well recognized, satire inflicts death in varying ways. In a well-known passage he remarks that

> there is still a vast difference betwixt the slovenly butcher-
> ing of a man, and the fineness of a stroke that separates the
> head from the body, and leaves it standing in its place. A

man may be capable, as Jack Ketch's wife said of his serv-
ant, of a plain piece of work, a bare hanging; but to make
a malefactor die sweetly was only belonging to her husband.

In this example, Dryden's image for satire is that of a minister
of justice, the public hangman. What is remarkable is that the
poet would like to apply the image of such a role and such a
skill to himself,

> if the reader would be kind enough to think it belongs to
> me. The character of Zimri in my *Absalom* is, in my opin-
> ion, worth the whole poem: 'tis not bloody, but 'tis ridicu-
> lous enough. And he for whom it was intended was too
> witty to resent it as an injury. If I had railed, I might have
> suffered for it justly: but I managed my own work more
> happily, perhaps more dexterously. I avoided the mention
> of great crimes, and applied myself to the representing of
> blindsides, and little extravagancies; to which, the wittier a
> man is, he is generally the more obnoxious [that is, vulner-
> able]. It succeeded as I wished; the jest went round, and he
> was laughed at in his turn who began the frolic.[36]

What a contrast, we feel, there is between the razor stroke and
that little "frolic" in Restoration England. We now know that
Zimri, or rather the Duke of Buckingham, had no such notion
that he had died sweetly. Awkward as they are, the verses that
he wrote down, "To Dryden," show as much.

> As witches images of man invent
> To torture those they're bid to represent,
> And as the true live substance does decay
> Whilst that slight idol melts in flames away,
> Such and no lesser witchcraft wounds my name,
> So thy ill-made resemblance wastes my fame.[37]

Not all satiric transformations are processes of degeneration
to death. I single out this form in order to heighten as far as

possible the contrary transforming modes of satire and panegyric. Here is the panegyric mode on death, again illustrated from Dryden.

> For ev'n when Death dissolves our Humane Frame, ⎤
> The Soul returns to Heav'n, from whence it came; ⎬
> Earth keeps the Body, Verse preserves the Fame.[38] ⎦

Panegyric transforms its object to life and immortality, whereas satire may be so extreme as to lead to death. Panegyric may be typified by the title of the collection celebrating Ben Jonson after his death, *Jonsonus Virbius,* for Virbius is the man who was revived from death to live twice. Satire moves from its implied ideal city or ideal person, or from the real city and historical man, to a foolish, evil counterpart. With fear and an enduring magic, satire possesses extraordinary force by bearing upon us our sense of loss and an unrelieved conviction that the degeneration should not be so.

Such an emphasis can lead to consideration of the ending of but one poem, the fourth book of *The Dunciad.* In it the dark night of Dulness and of death is universal.

> She comes! she comes! the sable Throne behold
> Of *Night* Primaeval, and of *Chaos* old!
> Before her, *Fancy*'s gilded clouds decay,
> And all its varying Rain-bows die away.
> *Wit* shoots in vain its momentary fires,
> The meteor drops, and in a flash expires. (IV, 629–634)

The effective verbs are relentless: *decay, die, expires.* And the world's epitaph is final.

> Lo! thy dread Empire, CHAOS! is restor'd;
> Light dies before thy uncreating word:
> Thy hand, great Anarch! lets the curtain fall;
> And Universal Darkness buries All. (IV, 653–656)

On Pope's sublime vision, the degeneration to death is meta-
physical, even apocalyptic.
Paradoxically, however, the final transformation of satire, like
that of any art, is into immortality. Immortal dying it no doubt
is, but such satiric art is one variety of the *ars bene moriendi*.
In it, Dr. Johnson's sentence upon a writer dull in life is belied
in satire by art's powers to transform. What is true of Sir Richard
Blackmore is not true of *The Dunciad*: "inherent and radical
dullness will never be much invigorated by extrinsick animation." [39] We have here a reminder that art and life are too complex in themselves and in their relation to each other to permit
us to accept the Elizabethan identification of the satire with the
character of the poet as Satyr; it is much too late in the day
to follow Macaulay in thinking our greatest English satiric poet
a monster. Pope's own last hours before real death included that
debility of mind that many of us can expect.

> Bolingbroke sometimes wept over him in this state of help-
> less decay, and being told by Spence that Pope, at the inter-
> mission of his deliriousness, was always saying something
> kind either of his present or absent friends, and that his
> humanity seemed to have survived his understanding, an-
> swered, "It has so." And added, "I never in my life knew
> a man that had so tender a heart for his particular friends,
> or more general friendship for mankind." At another time
> he said, "I have known Pope these thirty years, and value
> myself more in his friendship than—" his grief then sup-
> pressed his voice.[40]

Or as Congreve said, with touching simplicity, of another poet
sometimes typified as a satirist, "I loved Mr. *Dryden*." [41]
Satire possesses fearsome powers, but the satiric art employs a
rhetoric, that is, a choice of artistic means, just as do panegyric,
epic, and tragedy. In writing satire, a poet necessarily transforms
by choices, from a variety of alternatives, a part of himself and

of that great city that constitutes his imperfect world. And we must recognize that the greatest English satirists wear singing-robes as many-colored as Joseph's coat. Their art, and their lives, are vast, as Whitman said, and contain multitudes. Although Pope could write so convincingly and movingly of that "Universal Darkness," he had also written, less than a decade before, in one of the loveliest poetic phrases I know, of "The soul's calm sun-shine." [42] Unless I am wholly wide of the mark, both the dark and the bright vision of human life tell us something enduring about ourselves and testify to the various transforming powers of the highest poetic art.

Pope's
Illusive Temple of Infamy

Michael Rosenblum

INDIANA UNIVERSITY

One of the peculiarities of the modern sensibility is its admiration for works which are about themselves: poems about the writing of poetry, or even more familiar, novels about the writing (and the reading) of novels. We have known for a long time that *Tristram Shandy* is not an oddity, but only recently have we begun to think of it as in some ways the typical novel. A writer is self-conscious when he sees the activity in which he is engaged as problematic, and for us to be self-conscious seems to be more natural than to be unself-conscious. If this is true, then I think satire can legitimately lay claim to being a genre suited to the modern taste because it was self-conscious a long time before modern exercises in literary introversion became fashionable.[1] From its beginnings, satire has been considered problematic as moral activity and as art.

The lyric poet need not justify his impulse to song, but the satirist does because he seems to choose to sing of the deformed, the vicious, and the absurd. The traditional charge against the satirist is that he expresses his own pathology rather than the sickness that he claims to observe in the society around him. The satirist is a man with a bias, in some striking cases literally thrown off balance by curvature of the spine, a clubfoot, or affliction of the middle ear. A more psychologically acute version of this charge is that what the satirist pretends to discover in his target may well be a projection of the same vice within himself. Kenneth Burke observes that "the satirist attacks in others the weaknesses and temptations that are really within himself." Satire is then "an approach from without to something within." [2]

The satirist has ready answers for his critics, has in fact been elaborating and passing down a defense of his art to succeeding generations of satirists. According to his own self-portrait, he is the most moral of men, the sworn enemy of vice and folly, the doctor who purges and heals a sick society, the defender of civilization against its enemies. Moreover, he doesn't choose to write satire: faced with the spectacle of Augustan Rome or Augustan England or twentieth-century Los Angeles, and the energy and persistence of the knaves and fools who inhabit them, it is difficult not to write satire. As Pope says, "Fools rush into my head, and so I write." [3] The satirist finds it easy to don the robes of virtue—what in Pope's case Maynard Mack describes as the "now almost seamless garment formed of ancient Rome and Twickenham and seventeenth-century retirement precedents, which signalized the posture of the honest satirist protesting a corrupt society." [4]

Even if the satirist convinces us that his work is morally justified, there is still the question of whether it can be much good as art. According to a long tradition satire is the bastard genre, a farrago, a mixed dish, a hastily set down affair without the style and unity of the more elevated genres. Horace asks is it Lucillus' own fault or "his rugged themes that denied him smoothness?" (Satires I, X, 56-9), and Pope makes that question the epigraph

for his "versification" of Donne's satires. The answer often given
is that the genre itself makes attention to formal values difficult.
One doesn't refine and polish when the times demand a bold,
truthful voice. Moreover, the nature of the subject matter im-
poses limitations: the poet may know how to treat Aeneas, but
what if his subject is Curll or Colley Cibber? Speaking of the
epic games in Book II of *The Dunciad*, Pope points out that "if
we consider that the Exercises of his *Authors* could with justice
be no higher than *Tickling, Chatt'ring, Braying,* or *Diving,* it
was no easy matter to invent such Games as were proportion'd
to the meaner degree of *Booksellers* . . . with whom it had been
great impropriety to have joined any but vile ideas. . . ." [5]
Satire's decorum demands "vile ideas." The poet can only hope
that what Addison says of Virgil in *The Georgics* would be true
of him: he "tosses about his Dung with an air of Majesty."
Finally, how can a poem be expected to survive if it depends on
the reader's knowledge of particulars which are anything but
timeless? No matter, satire can be an inferior genre artistically
since morality is its primary concern. It is permissible for Lucillus' stream to be muddy. The satirist often even appears willing
to offer up his rough, fragmentary poem as evidence of his moral
seriousness. As Pope says, "Truth guards the Poet, sanctifies the
line, / And makes Immortal, Verse as mean as mine" (*Epilogue
to the Satires: Dialogue II*).

What satirists have said about themselves—that they are moral-
ists first and only incidentally artists—is reflected in scholarly
criticism of satire. According to this view, the satirist is really
a kind of rhetorician. No matter how distorted the satirist's fictions, no matter how obliquely he equates his fictional world
with the outside world, ultimately he is writing about something
which exists outside the frame of his own work, something that
"refers beyond the page" to a situation that has a historical basis
and which he wants us to condemn: Thus according to Sheldon

Sacks "a satire is a work organized so that it ridicules objects external to the fictional world created in it." Ronald Paulson argues that "however much mimesis or representation is involved, the generic end is rhetorical." [6]

If satire's reflexiveness, its concern with its own form, makes it seem like a genre congenial to modern taste, the rhetorical view of satire makes it seem old-fashioned in that it runs counter to a view of the relation of poetry to the real world that has become orthodox in many influential poetics. I'll use Northrop Frye's distinction between "ornamental speech" and "persuasive speech," but I think a similar distinction could be found in many other places. According to Professor Frye "ornamental speech" and "persuasive speech" are "psychologically opposed to each other, as the desire to ornament is essentially disinterested, and the desire to persuade is essentially the reverse. In fact ornamental rhetoric is inseparable from literature itself, or what we have called the hypothetical verbal structure which exists for its own sake. Persuasive rhetoric is applied literature, or the use of literary art to reinforce the power of argument. Ornamental rhetoric acts on its hearers statically, leading them to admire its own beauty or wit; persuasive rhetoric tries to lead them kinetically toward a course of action." [7] It seems clear to me that in the view of the critics I have been citing as well as some of the satirists themselves, satire is persuasive speech rather than ornamental speech. The satirist is interested in his work primarily for its power to move his audience; no matter how inventive the *personae* or ingenious the metaphors, these literary devices exist only to persuade the audience. This also means that the reader's response to satire is correspondingly changed. Instead of the disinterested contemplation of the work in all its internal relations, the appropriate response is to translate the fictions back into the world which they in some way comment upon (Grand Academy of Lagado = the Royal Society), and then if we are persuaded, we evaluate the outside object in a new light (empirical experiments = extracting sunbeams from cucumbers). We are denied the centripetal movement of a purer poetry, and are forced to shuttle back and forth between two realms.

It might be possible to say that Dickens' London is not, nor does it purport to be, the "real" London as it existed outside the novel, but rather a "vision" of London, incorporating some of the historically recognizable features of London, but existing in its own right. (Though to the extent that we might consider the Dickens of *Bleak House* a satirist, one might argue that we are meant to see that Chancery = the real Chancery). But we never could say the same of Pope's or Swift's London—its existence is not so self-contained; it takes its Cibbers and Theobalds from history, what Mack calls "the chronicle of the existing city." The dunces are not hypothetical constructs to be observed disinterestedly. It may be true that other poets never affirm anything and therefore never lie, but the satirist is affirming something, albeit negatively. The satirist's efforts are tied to history, "the existing city," in a way that other poets' efforts are not. Sidney's poet makes a second nature, ranges freely within the zodiac of his own wit, substituting for our brazen nature the golden world of his own invention; but the satirist must stick with the brazen one and try to make us feel its weight.

If he succeeds in making us feel its weight, then we might try to do something about it; the work will be "kinetic" and produce consequences in the real world. Another poet has said that poetry doesn't make anything happen in the world. But satire does—as in the case of *The Drapier's Letters,* which actually brought about the cancellation of Wood's patent. Satire tries to make us move back to the world; it may try to make us forget there are two realms. Paulson has argued that "as satire increases in rhetorical effectiveness it draws less and less attention to itself as satire; ultimately the most effective satire (given its generic aims) would be the one that passed as something else. (The reader's knowledge that he is reading satire makes him more aware of formal matters and less concerned about combatting evil.)"[8] He cites Swift's "Dying Statement" of Ebenezor Elliston, a counterfeit confession of a condemned criminal which threatened to expose those colleagues who did not reform. According to Walter Scott the crime rate of Dublin actually went down. The natural direction of satire then, "given its generic aims," is toward illusionism, the foisting of the art work into the real world. The satirist disappears as he tries to smuggle his creations into the real world. Swift disappears (taking Partridge along with him) and leaves Bickerstaff behind. The satirist has become what Hugh Kenner calls a counterfeiter, someone whose "real purpose is to efface himself, like the Flaubertian artist, so that we will draw the conclusion he wants us to about how his artifact came into existence."[9]

An even more radical and challenging account of the satirist's (or satire's) self-annihilating tendencies is provided by Edward Said's argument that for Swift the fact that a work survived as a literary text was a sign of its failure. Swift was interested in writing only as it is "stimulated by a specific occasion and planned in some way to change it. . . . Correct writing for him did not merely conform to reality. It was reality; or better still, it was an event necessitated by other events, and leading to still other events."[10] Success as an event "would have meant its extinction and dispersion in time past." If we can extend what Said says of Swift to all satire, then satire has only the most qualified reason for its existence: it is, on the one hand, a middle term suspended precariously between the causes outside itself, the occasions which have provoked it into existence, and on the other hand, the consequences or events which it is meant to provoke in the outside world. If the satirist feels that he can no longer change reality, make his art truly "kinetic," then he might as

well stop writing. In the footnote attached to the end of the
Epilogue to the Satires: Dialogue II, Pope claims that he resolves
to publish no more poems of the same kind. "Could he have
hoped to have amended any, he had continued these attacks. . . ." This little epilogue to the *Epilogue* might be considered the satirist's farewell to his art.

This seems to me as far as you can take the view that the
satirist is primarily a moralist, a rhetorician concerned with the
effects of his art on history. Before satire as a genre disappears
entirely, I would like to reverse the direction in which we have
been moving and pursue some of the implications of the opposing view: that satire is ornamental rhetoric rather than persuasive rhetoric, that it flaunts its own artifice rather than conceals it, and that it is concerned with the powers of the satirist
and the act of satire rather than with any situation which exists
outside the satire. In this view the satirist may pose as outraged
moralist, but that is only one of the conventional fictions of satire.
No matter what he may claim, the satirist is moved to write
satire for the same reason the lyric poet is moved to song; he is
not trying to explore the substantive issues of Ancients versus
Moderns, or the *Querelles des Femmes,* or the doctrines of
Leibniz. These serve only as the occasions for the poem, and as
an artist he is grateful to them. The Tory wits keep attacking all
the machinery of scholastic philosophy and logic not because they
see these ways of thinking as threats to society, but because they
realize that these vanishing enemies provide them with a perfect
opportunity for the display of their own kind of virtuosity. The
satirist doesn't really hate lawyers, quack doctors, pedant philosophers, braggart soldiers, antiquarians, opera singers, or even
bad poets—he just sees their artistic possibilities and is drawn to
them as the landscape painter is to picturesque waterfalls. If
this goes too far and replaces the moralist's toga with the formalist's velvet jacket, one might say that the satirist is "interested"

in these phenomena in the sense proposed by Austin Warren: "As its signal advantage, burlesque, (with its allied forms, satire and irony) allows a self-conscious writer to attend to objects, causes, and persons in which he is deeply interested, yet of which, in part or with some part of him, he disapproves. 'Interest' is a category which subsumes love and hate, approval and disapproval; often it is an unequal, an unsteady mixture." [11]

Where this is not the case, where the writer doesn't have the necessary detachment for the contemplation of his subject, where the man with a cause takes precedence over the artist, then the result is a work like *The History of John Bull*. The actual issues of the War of the Spanish Succession, the peace negotiations leading to the Treaty of Utrecht, the Union with Scotland are important to Arbuthnot, and so the fictions are threadbare and lifeless. Whatever the importance of the work for historians, for literature the work is dead, in much the same way that Smollett's *Adventures of an Atom* is dead. The rhetorician who wants to move his audience kinetically to action in the real world may use irony or metaphor, but only within limits: brilliant as they are, the polemics of Junius are too closely tied to history to be works of satire. When Swift really wanted to make something happen in the world, he was wise enough to play it fairly straight, leave out the fireworks of wit, and distort the issues only minimally. Hence *The Drapier's Letters*, which some critics would not consider satire.

If on the other hand we examine the great works of satire we will see how unrhetorical they really are. Good rhetoric is never unclear or ambiguous, but good satire can be—as the controversy (surely not all of it fabricated, not all the result of historical misunderstanding) over the "meaning" of Swift's masterpieces indicates. The rhetorician's "meaning" is thinner and more easily formulated, whereas the satirist's "meaning" in literature is dense.

Paulson in arguing for what I have called the rhetorical view
of satire has claimed that "Satire's purpose ordinarily is not to
create something new but to expose the real evil in the existing." [12] To that one might oppose what T. S. Eliot says of Ben
Jonson: "But satire like Jonson's is great in the end not by
hitting off its object, but by creating it; the satire is merely the
means which leads to the aesthetic result, the impulse which
projects a new world into a new orbit." [13] "A new world into a
new orbit," not the old world distorted for rhetorical purposes.
The satirist doesn't transform our brazen world upward into a
golden world like other poets, but downward into an equally
autonomous, equally aesthetic world of lead.

If the first view of satire led ultimately to the disappearance
of the satirist and his art, the second ushers both back again in
full glory. I think the possibility of reversing direction has been
implicit in the notion of counterfeiting and illusionism. The
point about counterfeiting, if I understand Kenner's argument,
is that for the wise reader it implies a counterfeiter. We look for
traces of the controlling person, the real author, who is not counterfeit—Swift, not Bickerstaffe. A real author is a presence, a
live voice, and thus for Pope and Swift, different from the dead
voices which surround them. I think the same is true of illusionism in art: it is easy to see that *trompe l'oeil* painting always
calls attention to itself as artifice, as a triumph of the painter's
art. It's only crows who try to peck at grapes. And it is only the
gulls that get taken in by Swift's labyrinth peopled with mock
Partridges. For the ones who share the irony, the men of wit
and taste to whom Swift appeals in the Preface to *A Tale of a
Tub*, the interest is in the maker of the maze. The real object is
not to discredit Partridge so much as to show what the ingenious
satirist can accomplish. For all their evasiveness, their impostures,
the fictions of *Gulliver's Travels*, *A Tale of a Tub*, and *The*

Dunciad return us to the figure of the satirist at work on the poem.

All this by way of introduction to *The Dunciad,* a work which culminates Pope's career, and which also brings to fulfillment the Scriblerean program of compiling the complete works of the unlearned. That project was first adumbrated in *A Tale of a Tub,* a panegyric upon modernism by an "author" whose other productions also anticipate *The Dunciad: A Character of the Present Wits in this Island, A Dissertation upon the Principal Productions of Grub Street,* and *A Description of the Kingdom of Absurdities.* In *The Art of Sinking in Poetry* Pope acknowledged "the extent, Fertility, and Populousness of our Lowlands of Parnassus" by codifying that realm's poetics, but it wasn't until *The Dunciad in Four Books* of 1743 that the comprehensive and definitive account of all the works of dullness was achieved. It may be also argued that *The Dunciad* is a culminating work of the satirist's art, a virtuoso demonstration of how the apparent limitations of the genre can be converted to artistic gain. *The Dunciad* is a work about dunces, but it is also a work about *The Dunciad.* It reveals satire's peculiar combination of private motivation and disinterestedness, moral rhetoric and autonomous poetry. It shows how the satirist may efface himself or assert his presence, how he can make his poem and the world interact, and how he can make a beautiful and enduring poem out of the ugly and transient materials with which he is forced to deal.

If, as Dr. Johnson informs us, Pope could make the taking of tea an occasion for stratagem, we shall not be surprised if the making of *The Dunciad* calls forth all the poet's "indirect and unsuspected methods." *The Dunciad* is an illusive poem in every way, a mocking, jeering, apparition intended to deceive the mental eye by its false prospects. Pope disorients the reader by misleading him about the work's mode of existence. A poem may be described with reference to four coordinates: the work itself, its author, the audience, and what M. H. Abrams, whose scheme I am borrowing, calls "the universe." The work has "a subject which directly or deviously is derived from existing things." [14] Pope constantly shifts and plays upon each of these coordinates and their possible relationships, so that the limits of each term become something of a puzzle. This is the kind of serious game exploring the boundaries between art and reality that writers of our own time have liked to play, but as Kenner shows in *The Counterfeiters,* it is a game which Pope and Swift had perfected in the first half of the eighteenth century.

It is not so easy to decide what the term "the work itself" refers to when we speak of *The Dunciad.* Certainly Pope's contemporary reader was bound to be puzzled by the status of a poem ushered or smuggled into the world in such a way as to produce anger or amusement depending on the nature of the reader. The physical text itself—what should be the most substantial aspect of the work—proves to be a phantom. The title page of the first edition claims that it is a London reprint of a prior Dublin edition, but that edition never existed. It bears the name of a publisher who did exist, but who probably had nothing to do with the publication of the poem. The publisher's preface "prefixed to the first five imperfect editions of the *Dunciad in Three Books,*" the first item in the appendix to *The Dunciad Variorum,* admits that the publication is unauthorized: "How I came possest of it, [the manuscript] is no concern of the Reader. . . . If it provoke the Author to give us a more perfect edition, I have my end" (pp. 203–204). The advertisement to the first separate edition of the *Fourth Book of the Dunciad* is even less reassuring about the text: "It was found merely by accident, in taking a survey of the *Library* of a late eminent nobleman; but in so blotted a condition, and in so many detatch'd pieces, as plainly shewed it to be not only *incorrect,* but *unfinish'd*" (pp. 410–411). That is, the contemporary reader, having access only to corrupt or possibly pirated editions of an unfinished poem, would have to regard what he was reading as only the roughest approximation of the poet's intention. The repeated notices that there is more to come force him to anticipate a newer, more up-to-date *Dunciad.* As early in the poem as the preface of Martin Scriblerus we are warned that the crowd scene in the second book indicates "the design to be more extensive than to bad poets only, and that we may expect other Episodes . . . as occasion shall bring them forth" (p. 51). The poem is a potential poem, a work in progress as the original title *The Progress of Dulness* suggests, a design in the head of its creator; that design extends to parts of the poem yet to be written which will incorporate events in the outside world which have not yet taken place.

The modern reader can of course assume that there is no forthcoming completer *Dunciad,* but he is forced to cope with all the versions of the poem—*The Dunciad* of 1728, *The Dunciad Variorum* of 1729, the *New Dunciad* of 1742, and *The Dunciad in Four Books* of 1743 as well as all the many revisions, insertions, and deletions that took place in intervening editions. He also has the additional burden, as Pope knew he would, of trying to separate the mock–critical apparatus from the genuine critical apparatus of his scholarly editors. (In a letter he refers to "my *Chef d'ouevre,* the Poem of Dulness, which after I am dead and gone, will be printed with a large Commentary, and lettered on the back, *Pope's Dulness.*")[15] All of this makes *The Dunciad* a remarkably difficult poem to possess. I don't think that one can argue that since *The Dunciad* of 1743 represents Pope's final intentions, it supplants the earlier versions. Pope wants the reader to remember that there were earlier versions as he reads the last one, since the notes often refer to changes which have been made. Cibber's throne has only recently been vacated by Theobald, whom "we have ordered . . . utterly to vanish, and evaporate out of this work" (p. 252). (But this "Notice" is posted conspicuously at the very beginning of the poem lest the reader forget Theobald.) Although that progress is now complete, the poem is still a progress of Dullness, and the multiple versions of the poem (*Dunciad A* to *Dunciad B* in the Twickenham edition) are meant to record and enact that process, just as it is enacted in any one version of the poem.

Authorship is something of a mystery—not the minor mystery of who actually wrote the poem (that was solved almost immediately despite Pope's half-hearted but necessary attempts to conceal his authorship), but rather how our notion of authorship must be enlarged to account for a work which seems to accumulate by means of a continuing collaboration between the poet, his friends, his enemies, and anyone else who reads the poem and wishes to join in. William Cleland's letter to the publisher, which first appeared in the quarto of 1729 and remained a part of the work thereafter, invites the publisher to keep adding to the text: "Such Notes as have occurr'd to me I herewith send you; you will oblige me by inserting them amongst those which are, or will be, transmitted to you by others: since not only the Author's friends, but even strangers, appear ingag'd by humanity, to some care of an orphan of so much genius and spirit, which its parent seems to have abandoned from the very beginning, and suffered to step into the world naked, unguarded, and unattended" (p. 11). The invitation is extended to any reader in the advertisement to *New Dunciad* of 1742:

> If any person be possessed of a more perfect copy of this work, or any other fragments of it, and will communicate them to the publisher, we shall make the next edition more complete: In which, we also promise to insert any *Criticisms* that shall be published (if at all to the purpose) with the *Names* of the *Authors;* or any Letters sent us (tho' not to

the purpose) shall yet be printed under the title of *Epistolæ
Obscurorum Virorum;* which, together with some others of
the same kind formerly laid by for that end, may make no
unpleasant addition to the future impressions of this poem.[16]

As Sutherland points out this last invitation satirizes Curll's
methods of publication. But the invitation also indicates Pope's
method of building up the poem by "over-dubbing" a babble of
real and mock voices: Martinus Scriblerus, Bentley of the face-
tious notes, those puppets through which the "two or three of
my friends" [17] who Pope claims wrote the notes speak (but who
are probably in turn puppets through which Pope speaks), the
puppet voice of William Cleland,[18] through which Pope delivered an impassioned justification of himself, the semi-puppet
"Warburton" used for more solemn effects, and most of all the
voices of dunces as they respond to Pope's invitation or as gleaned
from their own writings.

Pope wants to distance himself from the poem in order that
the true "voice" of *The Dunciad* will not be the angry, maligned
poet, but a more impersonal one, resonant and authoritative
above the din of dissonant mock-voices that sound in the poem
and the notes. This does not disguise the fact that *The Dunciad*
is among other things a monumental paying off of scores, as
Pope admits when he writes to Swift that "this poem will rid
me of these insects" (2, 481, March 23, 1728). At the same time,
Pope's efforts at removing his presence from the poem are balanced by his wish to assert his presence. The passage I just quoted
in which "Cleland" describes the poem as an orphan "which its
parent seems to have abandoned from the very beginning and
suffered to step into the world naked, unguarded, and unattended" illustrates Pope's ambiguous relation to the poem: instead of being an orphan, the poem is more like the beloved
child whom the parent only pretends to relinquish, the better
to supply his offspring with stepparents, sponsors, and guardians

to see it safely into the world and protect it when the parent is no longer on the scene. Hence Pope repeatedly makes Swift another father of the poem: "Do you care I shou'd say anything farther how much the poem is yours?" [19] He makes use of the indispensable noble lords to take the responsibility for the patent, and after the immediate danger is over replaces them with the printer Lawton Gilliver. Later on, William Warburton is solicited to become editor, contributor to, and protector of the poem: "I have a particular reason to make you Interest yourself in Me and My Writings. It will cause both them and me to make the better figure to Posterity" (4, 428, November 27, 1742). Far from being an abandoned orphan, the satire is a continuing presence in the poet's life, and eventually becomes his claim upon posterity.

The poet seems to withdraw from the work, but as in the case of Cleland's letter (it is Pope who writes it), he is most there when he seems to have disappeared. This seems to me a characteristic stance of the satirist, who often deprecates his own importance by asserting that writing a satire is only making a response to an occasion. Thus Pope claims that the "late Flood of Slander" which resulted from the publication of *The Peri-Bathos* "gave birth to *The Dunciad*." The enthronement of Cibber in the 1743 version would in the same way appear to be a response to Cibber's publication in 1742 of *A Letter from Mr. Cibber to Mr. Pope*. But both events, the actions of the dunces and Cibber, may very well have been engineered by Pope himself, who not only anticipated their response, but may have actually provoked it to justify the poem.[20] If one of the occasions of *The Dunciad* is the "uncontrolled License of the Press" and the "Late Flood of Slander," then it is a flood which, at least in part, the poet has instigated. Granted that Cibber and the dunces exist out there in the universe, the poet can nevertheless manipulate events to serve an artistic purpose. The satirist pretends to be taking candid snapshots from life, but practices instead a very highly contrived portraiture: he tricks his subjects into striking the poses in which they are captured within the poem.

Pope is, at his most oblique and ingenious, a practitioner of "indirect and unsuspected methods" in his deliberate complication of the relation between his poem and the universe, the characters and events of history to which the poem refers. Is it "document," the record of the artist's confrontation of his historical situation in order to shape the reader's response to that situation, or is it "monument," "a richly solipsistic or playful edifice?"[21] The aspect of the poem that concerns me now is the surprising way in which it can serve as an illustration of both extreme views of satire. Pope makes the question of satire's capacity to mirror history or to mirror itself one of the important issues of the poem.

The Dunciad would seem to be the perfect example of how far a satirist can go in aligning his poem with history. If ever a poem could be said to be "the chronicle of the existing city," the record of the literary and political world of London in the first half of the eighteenth century, it is *The Dunciad*—or so the satirist would have us believe. The poet may falsify information or he may reveal his biases in politics, but the fact that he offers a *version* of history doesn't alter our sense that his conception of the poem is historical. In fact the poet is so concerned that his work and outside events be aligned that he is willing to keep changing his poem so that it will keep up with history. If someone dies, or makes his peace with Pope or quarrels with him, or if Sir Thomas Hamner has a new edition of Shakespeare ready for the presses, these new developments must somehow be registered by the poem, by an insertion, by a new footnote, or an addition to an existing footnote, or by a new version of the poem. Lines 115-118 in Book IV appear with the following note: "These four lines were printed in a separate leaf by Mr. Pope in the last edition, which he himself gave, of the Dunciad, with

directions to the printer, to put this leaf into its place as soon
as Sir T. H.'s Shakespear should be published" (p. 352–3). Lines
247–250 in A, Book I read: "Know, Settle, cloy'd with custard
and with praise, / Is gather'd to the Dull of antient days, / Safe,
where no criticks damn, no duns molest, / Where Gildon, Banks,
and high-born Howard rest" (p. 92). In editions of A from
1735c–1742 there is an additional couplet: "And high-born *Howard*, more majestic sire, / Impatient waits, till ** grace the quire"
(p. 92). The ranks of the dull of ancient days received some dis-
tinguished additions in the years that intervened between *Dunciad
A* and *Dunciad B*: Eusden died in 1730, Ned Ward in 1731,
and best and most recent of all, Lord Hervey in 1743, just in time
for a last minute change in the text. Thus the corresponding
lines in *Dunciad B*, Book I, lines 293–298, read:

> Know, Eusden thirsts no more for sack or praise;
> He sleeps among the dull of ancient days;
> Safe, where no Critics damn, no duns molest,
> Where wretched Withers, Ward, and Gildon rest,
> And high-born Howard, more majestic sire,
> With Fool of Quality compleats the quire. (p. 291)

If somebody makes a suitable act of submission to Pope he can
be taken out of the poem, as in the case of the poet originally
referred to in *Dunciad A,* III, line 146. The footnote to that
line informs us how one can disappear from *The Dunciad*: "But
the person who suppos'd himself meant applying to our author
in a modest manner, and with declarations of his innocence, he
removed the occasion of his uneasiness. At the same time 'prom-
ising to do the like to any other who could give him the same
assurance, of having never writ scurrilously against him'" (pp.
162–163). If you can get out of the poem, you can also be dragged
into it, as in the case of Arnall, who was originally to have a
place in the poem but who managed to talk Pope into omitting

his name. He appears in a later version because "since, by the most unexampled insolence, and personal abuse of several great men, the Poet's particular friends, he most amply deserved a niche in the Temple of Infamy . . ." (p. 312). The contents of the poem, what is to be included or omitted, is dictated not by inner logic and the organic form of the whole, but simply by the course of events in the world, in this case a minor literary figure's present state of grace with the poet. *The Dunciad* is not a necessary whole whose integrity is inviolable; on the contrary it is the only masterpiece of literature whose contents are negotiable.

If the poem is to be tied to external events in this way, then it must necessarily be incomplete. Pope can no more finish his poem than Tristram Shandy can complete the account of his life. Just as the novelist discovers more circumstances that demand treatment, so the satirist is besieged by new specimens of dullness. The fiction of succession within the poem allows new versions to be written: Dunce the second reigns like Dunce the first; the line stretches backward into the past, and also into the future. There will always be new claimants for the throne. There are new recognition scenes to be enacted as Dullness acknowledges her own, and in turn, her own loyal sons acknowledge her. More activities, especially those in the world of politics,[22] are revealed to be inspired by Dullness, just as her sway extends over more and more of London, England, and Europe, until finally she does as prophesied embrace the whole world. The Cibber enthronement does not really seem a new direction in the poem, but rather a natural evolution of the fiction of succession, which allows for multiple Dunciads. We know that poets often revise poems making them better or worse, or that poets can write sequels to their own poems, but it is difficult to think of a continuing poem like *The Dunciad* which has to be revised, expanded, and updated to take into account the rush of events in the outside world.

But the claim to historical authenticity is an illusion. No matter how much the poem and footnotes seem to refer to history, to reflect a subject which "is derived from existing things," that is only one of the fictions of the poem. On this point I can only repeat Aubrey Williams' argument that in the notes Pope systematically displaces history. The dunces are placed in "a curiously ambiguous realm of half-truth in which the reader wanders, never quite sure as to the validity of what he reads, never certain what is fact, what is make-believe." [23] The poem "simultaneously affirms and denies its historical connections at every moment . . ." (p. 76). "The Tibbald of *The Dunciad* is not quite the Theobald of history" (p. 68). Of course the duncial don't know that, and so they send in indignant corrections which are incorporated into the next edition of the poem. Curll protests that he stood in the pillory not in March but February, and was moreover tossed in a rug, not a blanket. Ned Ward claims that it is not true that he keeps a public house in the City—rather he sells Port in Moor-Fields. The dull are troubled that Cibber's brazen, brainless brothers are made out of wood and therefore should be called "blocks"; they worry whether Theobald really was supperless, or whether the statement that Curll's "rapid waters in their passage burn" did actually "convey an idea of what was said to be Mr. Curll's condition at that time."

What the wise reader sees (and like other Scriblerean works, *A Tale of a Tub* and *The Bickerstaffe Papers,* the work has multiple aspects according to the nature of its audience) [24] is that the dunces are only raw material for a poem. They don't occasion the poem so much as become occasions for the exercise of the satirist's art. Pope everywhere asserts the priority of the poem over history:

> For whoever will consider the Unity of the whole design,
> will be sensible, that the *Poem was not made for these
> Authors, but these Authors for the Poem:* And I should

judge they were clapp'd in as they rose, fresh and fresh, and chang'd from day to day, in like manner as when the old boughs wither, we thrust new ones into a chimney. (Appendix I pp. 205–206)

For all their noise and activity, the dunces are mute and passive, completely subject to the "design" of the poet, who is free to paste them in, tear them out, or shuffle them about in the niches or slots that the poem contains. He manipulates them in accord with the internal logic of the poem, and is perfectly free to ignore their "historical" identity. Thus line 118 in Book II of *Dunciad A* is "Breval, Besaleel, Bond, the Varlets caught" (p. 111), and in the corresponding line in *Dunciad B* it is "Breval, Bond, Besaleel, the varlets caught" (p. 301). Prosody is all. A line in which asterisks are used to indicate the name of a dunce suddenly is altered to include the name of the dunce, and the name is "Concanen." The note attached to that line explains that "this name was since inserted merely to fill up the verse, and give ease to the ear of the reader." [25]

Lines prepared for any dunce can be applied to any other dunce. If Bentley can be moved into a slot originally intended for Welsted ("Welsted his mouth with classic flatt'ry opes" A II. l. 197 [p. 124] becomes "Bentley his mouth with classic flatt'ry opes" B II, 205 [p. 305]), then Welsted in turn can get the line previously occupied by Oldmixon, with only a slight adjustment needed for the extra syllable in Oldmixon's name: "But Oldmixon the Poet's healing balm" (p. 125) becomes "But Welsted most the Poet's healing balm" (p. 306). This aspect of the poem disturbed Dr. Johnson, who thought it didn't make sense to pretend that you can say the same thing of different men.[26] This is of course the point: the switch from Cibber to Theobald can be accomplished with a minimum of fuss, because like all the other dunces, they are really all the same. Going from Theobald to Cibber is only the distance from "Now

flames old Memnon, now Rodrigo burns" (A I, 208, p. 87) to
"Now flames the Cid, and now Perolla burns" (B I, 250, p. 288).
One need not respect their individuality because they have
none: they are "phantoms," "Things," fictions: "Reader! These
also are not real persons. . . . Thou mays't depend on it no such
authors ever lived: all phantoms" (p. 111). There were complaints about the chronology of the poem because the Gazetteers who are depicted had not "lived within the time of the
poem." Scriblerus replies that "we may with equal assurance
assert, these Gazetteers not to have lived since, and challenge
all the learned world to produce one such paper at this day.
Surely therefore, where the point is so obscure, our author
ought not to be censured too rashly" (p. 311). In the same way
Bickerstaffe had dismissed the question of the existence of
Partridge as a "point merely speculative" in a scholarly argument.

By responding to the "random" initials in *The Art of Sinking*
they have confessed their own fictionality, and thus the poet
"had acquired such a peculiar right over their Names as was necessary to his design" (p. 202). According to Ricardus Aristar-
chus, Cibber has made the same mistake in acknowledging that
he was in *The Dunciad*: "For no sooner had the fourth book
laid open the high and swelling scene, but he recognized his own
heroic Acts" (p. 261). Cibber has claimed that he would always
be a buffoon and so "he is become *dead in law,* (I mean the *law
Epopæian*) and descendeth to the Poet as his property: who may
take him, and deal with him, as if he had been dead as long as
an old Egyptian hero; that is to say, *embowel* and *embalm him
for posterity*" (p. 265). All the other dunces are dead in the same
way and therefore fit subjects for the satirist to make of them
what he will.

There is no point in trying to reconstruct the poem as history
since the events and figures with which it deals are so ephemeral,

and therefore in a way unreal. "Reality" may be better recorded and interpreted by reading the poem, which is a full and sufficient account of history. Not only is the poem aligned with history; in some instances it anticipates history. Thus line 146 of A III reads: "Lo Horneck's fierce, and Roome's funereal face" (p. 162). According to the note that accompanies the line, "These two are worthily coupled, being both virulent Party-writers; and one wou'd think prophetically, since immediately after the publishing of this Piece the former dying, the latter succeeded him in *Honour* and *Employment*" (p. 163). Another instance of prophecy is the couplet in A III associating two poets: "Beneath his reign, shall Eusden wear the Bays, / Cibber preside Lord-Chancellor of Plays" (pp. 186–187). The note comments: "I have before observ'd something like Prophecy in our Author. Eusden, whom he couples with Cibber, no sooner died but his place of Laureate was supply'd by Cibber, in the year 1730 . . ." (p. 187). Prophecy is not difficult since history is so predictable, a repetition of the same kinds of events; one knows that Philips or Cibber will be promoted for wit. Thus the poem can exhaust history. If the reader takes the trouble to keep up with the dunces, he will still not be enlightened, "since when he shall have found them out, he will probably know no more of the Persons than before" (p. 206). The conjunction of Horneck and Roome, of Eusden and Cibber conveys all the essential information about each, and history can only confirm the poet's intuition. The Lord Hervey of history is unimportant; it is only when he completes the quire, enters the pages of Pope's book, that he has any significance. Pope and the reader are not interested in who the dunce is, but only in what can be made of him. This seems to me the general issue in *The Dunciad*: how may the deeds of dullness be converted into an act of wit?

Doctor Johnson was not impressed by Pope's grotto; he thought it vain of the poet to pretend to have "extracted an ornament from an inconvenience." But perhaps the knack of extracting an ornament from an inconvenience is one of the qualifications of the satirist. Pope writes to Swift that he hopes Ambrose Philips will be promoted: "If they do not promote him, they'l spoil a very good conclusion to one of my Satyrs, where having endeavoured to correct the taste of the town in wit, and criticisme, I end thus: But what avails to lay down rules for Sense? / In ———'s reign these fruitless lines were writ, / When Ambrose Philips was preferr'd for wit!" (2, 332, October 15, 1725). Swift replied with the same resigned irony: "I would have the Preferment Just enough to save your lines; let it be ever so low, for your sake we will allow it to be Preferment" (2, 343, November 26, 1725). If you live in George's reign, and know that the lines must therefore be fruitless, the best you can do is to incorporate that couplet into a vast and intricate structure.

Relatively early in Pope's career he wrote a poem called *The Temple of Fame,* like *The Dunciad* a poem in which the poet is granted a vision. In the early poem, however, the poet celebrates those names which "From Time's first Birth, with Time it self shall last; / These ever new, nor subject to Decays, / Spread, and grow brighter with the Length of Days" (*Temple of Fame,* ll. 49–52). In a footnote to lines 178 through 243 Pope says that these great names were "describ'd in such Attitudes as express their different Characters. The Columns on which they are rais'd are adorn'd with Sculptures, taken from the most striking Subjects of their Works; which Sculpture bears a Resemblance in its Manner and Character, to the Manner and Character of their Writings" (p. 179). When some ten years later Pope decided that the times demanded a *Temple of Infamy,* he was able to use the same method to celebrate those whose names were already forgotten. The satirist is one who knows the ornamental value of grotesque sculpture when heroic sculpture is no longer possible.

The epigraph which Pope attaches to the title page of *Dunciad B* is from *The Metamorphoses* (XI, 58–60). After Orpheus has been slain by the wild women, the musician's head drifts out to the open sea still singing. A monster gets ready to pierce its lips and eyes but "Phoebus was quicker, for as the snake's tongue flickered / He glazed the creature into polished stone, / And there it stayed, smiling wide-open-jawed."[27] If I'm not being too heavy-handed about this, Orpheus is the maligned Pope, the monster the potentially dangerous Grubs, or Dullness herself at her moment of triumph. Phoebus is the power of poet, in this case "the power of satire," or more specifically the Pope who writes *The Dunciad*. The monster is transformed by the poem into an artifact, a piece of living statuary; though the original menace presented by the gaping jaws still shows clearly, the monster is now harmless. By the writing of *The Dunciad* the dull and their works are absorbed into a witty structure, a frame is put around chaos, and the apparent disorder of the dunces is revealed in the end to be a part of the poet's overarching design.

The poem itself celebrates the triumph of Dullness, but the making of the poem, the outside frame which is contributed by the notes and the fictional situation which they imply, suggests the forces of wit which are to contain Dullness. The poet has complete control over the dunces; like Prospero[28] he can decide who is going to be made to dance through the horseponds, or who, like Aaron Hill, will be allowed to jump out of the poem. The notes and appendices are joyfully accumulated by the poet and the partly imaginary circle of wits who are allied with him. The satirist is able to respond to any external circumstance: the corrections and protests of the dull, the false readings supplied by Curll and Concanen, a pirated edition—all these are incorporated into the next edition of the poem. The dunces are helpless and their works are fast disappearing: "As for their writings, I have sought them (on this one occasion) in vain, in the closets and libraries of all my acquaintance" ("A Letter to the Publisher," p. 14). The excerpts from the dunce's works which are made a part of the poem are all "that could be saved from the general destruction of such works." "Of the *Persons* it was judg'd proper to give some account; for since it is only in this monument that they must expect to survive, (and here survive they will, as long as the English tongue shall remain such as it was in the reigns of Queen ANNE and King GEORGE) it seem'd but humanity to bestow a word or two upon each, just to tell what he was, what he writ, when he liv'd, or when he dy'd" ("Advertisement," p. 8). The poem expresses the wish that the vanishing dunces and their equally ephemeral works be significant only in that they are a part of a poem which is not disappearing, but which is in fact multiplying and permanent. The works of the dunces are lost, but new versions of *The Dunciad* are found. The historical situation with which the poem deals is blotted out by *The Dunciad,* which transforms the threatening situation, the monster, the inconvenience of the historical pressure of the dunces into a work of art.

At the end of the *Temple of Fame* the "youthful bard" acknowledges that he too is "a candidate for praise." But he insists that he only seeks "an honest fame," the kind of fame which would seem to be difficult for a satirist to attain:

> Or if no Basis bear my rising Name,
> But the fall'n Ruins of Another's fame:
> Then teach me, heav'n! to scorn the guilty Bays;
> Drive from my Breast that wretched lust of Praise;
> Unblemish'd let me live, or die unknown,
> Oh grant an honest Fame, or grant me none! (p. 188)

The poet of *The Dunciad* has found a way to deal with the scruples of the youthful bard. The older (and cleverer) poet has discovered that the "fall'n ruins of another's fame" can make a very fine foundation for his own constructions. If not entirely "unblemished" the artful poet can at least avoid "the guilty bays." He can combine the negative and positive enterprise, make one edifice serve as Temple of Infamy for his enemies and a temple of fame for himself.

One last qualification: I have argued that Pope tries to substitute the poem for history, to transcend the occasions which have provoked the poem by means of making the poem. In this respect *The Dunciad* is a document, a record of Pope's sense of his situation in history. But if the poem expresses the wish that Dullness can be controlled, it also expresses the anxiety that Dullness cannot be contained by the poem. Even when the poet sounds most secure he reveals his doubt: *The Dunciad* is to be a monument which will survive "as long as the English tongue shall remain such as it was in the reigns of Queen ANNE and King GEORGE," but as Sutherland points out, Pope had strong doubts about the permanence of the English language. Is the vision recorded in Book III a chimera of the dreamer's brain, a vision passing through the Ivory gate, and thus "wild, ungrounded, and fictitious?" Or is the prophecy already coming true "in the writings of some even of our most adored authors, in Divinity, Philosophy, Physics, Metaphysics, etc. . . ."? (p. 192). Pope had ended poems with visions of the fall of a city before, but in the Horatian poems the poet has, to quote Professor Mack, "a place to stand, an angle of vision," the secure terrain provided by the garden and the grotto. But in *The Dunciad* the poet is less insulated; he may not be protected from the powers that he is ironically celebrating: "Ye Pow'rs! whose Mysteries restor'd I sing, / To whom Time bears me on his rapid wing, / Suspend a while your Force inertly strong, / Then take at once the Poet and the Song" (pp. 339–340). Is the vision of Dullness contained within the head of the poet, or is the poet contained within Dullness—is it Alice's dream or the Red King's? [29] The satirist may explore the abyss to show us what may happen if we stray too far, but once having taken us there, he may find it difficult to lead us out of it: it may be difficult to show that compared to the universal madness that is the human condition in "The Digression on Madness," or the universal dullness that is celebrated in *The Dunciad,* the life of common forms, of wit, order, and civilization are still possible, and thus exempt from the satirist's negative vision.[30]

Swift: The View from within the Satire

Ernest Tuveson
UNIVERSITY OF CALIFORNIA, BERKELEY

Jonathan Swift, to his own age and for subsequent generations, became in the popular estimation "The Satirist" almost as Shakespeare is established as "The Dramatist." In what way was Swift different from many other greatly gifted exemplars of the satiric imagination, who have never achieved his nigh-legendary status? Largely, I believe, not because of absolutely superior literary merit, but because his satire *works* more successfully than does the others'; that is to say, it touches the reader, even reaches out and grips him in spite of himself. For Swift's reputation is not one of affection. Indeed, probably, most readers would prefer to avoid looking into his satirical glass. Perhaps it will be useful to look again at the career of this master, *the* master of the satiric art; does it reveal the secret of his success?

In *A Tale of a Tub* and its companion works Swift made his debut as a satirist, and, in the view of some of us at least, wrote the supreme works of pure satirical imagination of his life. The *Tale* belongs to an older form of satire, that of the

55

Renaissance—learned, brilliant and exhibiting an endlessly varied
wit, the author constantly moving from one vantage point to another and constantly varying rhetorical technique. Although it
might have some influence on the general climate of opinion,
making informed readers more sensitive to frauds and follies in
religion and philosophy, its main function seems to be to delight
the rational imagination with its dazzling display. Is the author
really a fully realized *persona*? I come more and more to think
he is rather a voice, an alter ego of Swift himself (despite, of
course, obvious but not very important differences in their immediate conditions). The parallels with the author's own un-
certain future at this time are unmistakable: the wit's part is
certainly one Swift *could* have taken. He is, he says, performing
the "office of a wit," which is ironically described as contributing
to the repose as well as the diversion of the reader, whose "office"
in turn is to be full of "modern charity and tenderness." There
is an impression of author and reader engaging in an ingenious
game, trying to catch each other out, but ultimately sharing a
superior laugh at the diverting antics of their contemporaries;
and the exposure of Temple's critics, a stuffy bunch generally,
furnished much of the entertainment. Having identified himself
as a professional wit, the author could change his stance again
and again, without warning. The character of a "wit" was
recognized. Thus Dryden stated that

> . . . it is easier to write wit than humour; because in the
> characters of humour, the Poet is confin'd to make the
> person speak only what is proper to it. Whereas all kind of
> wit is proper to the Character of a witty person.[1]

There is, then, theoretically almost unlimited latitude for the
"witty person"—how much more so when he puts on the cap
and bells of the jester to the intellectual world! Yet Dryden goes
on to warn "that latitude would be of small advantage to such

Poets who have too narrow imagination to write it." The young Swift, intensely ambitious, took up this severe challenge. Yet there is some qualification even to the license allowed a wit: thus, Dryden says, a witty coward is differentiated from a witty brave. So the author of *A Tale* may be characterized, roughly, as an ironic allegorist and a panegyrist. He will shortly publish, it is reported, "A Panegyric upon the World" and "A Panegyrical Essay upon the Number THREE"; with a wink at the reader, he constantly protests his entire pleasure with the present order of things, which he ironically praises for what are in reality its faults; he protests he has not "a grain of satire" in his treatise. There may be a clue which we have missed. The word "panegyric" has as one of its accepted meanings a pejorative definition. It was solemnly described, without a grain of irony, in an early word book, as a "licentious kinde of speaking or oration, in the praise and commendation of Kings, or other great persons, wherein some falsities are joyned with many flateries." [2] Another word book likewise defines "panegyricall" as "spoken flatteringly in praise of some great person." [3] A few years later, the much-reprinted *The Gentleman Instructed* . . . , referring to fashionable men of the world, says:

> Who are those Men that awe us? A club of Animals, that have more Money than Wit and more Quality than Conscience; a pack of Hectors, that live ill, and judge worse; . . . the very Panegyricks of these Men are Satyrs, Praise out of their Mouths is scandalous. . . . [4]

Persons, that is to say, much like the charter members of the Academy the author of *A Tale* says is shortly to be established. So "panegyric" had, so to speak, already fixed connotations that established its ironic significance in satire; and the point may be relevant to later works of Swift as well.

But if *A Tale of a Tub* and *The Battle of the Books* brilliantly warranted Swift's literary credentials, they suggested some-

thing more. There can be detected a kind of disguised mani-
festo, a hint to the perceptive of a program for the future: a self-
imposed challenge great indeed. Although denying that he is
of a satirical disposition, the author laments that the "materials
of panegyric being very few in number have long since been
exhausted." [5] How little scope is there for an "honest satirist"!
But the materials for satire are endlessly fruitful, and the satirist
has achieved an enviable popularity; the implication is that, if
the author is to get out of his garret, here is the way. Indeed,
"Nature herself has taken order, that fame and honour should
be purchased at a better pennyworth, by satire, than by any other
productions of the brain; the world being soonest provoked to
praise by lashes, as men are to love." The parallel of erotic
masochism and what might be called satirical masochism is sug-
gestive; and may there not be a vaguely erotic effect in at least
some satire? It seems to be a danger Swift is determined to
avoid. All in all, here certainly is a curious state of affairs. Satire,
which should chastise and vex, which should be the most re-
sented of all literary productions, has become in fact the most
popular. For "being levelled at all," it is natural that "every
individual person makes bold to understand it of others."

There is much more to this effect, so much more that statements to this tenor loom large in the whole work (a little noted
point). In England you may assert (the reference of course is to
Donne) that "knavery and atheism are epidemic as the pox;
that honesty is fled with Astraea, and any other commonplaces
equally new and eloquent" and "the whole audience, far from
being offended, shall return you thanks as a deliverer of precious
and useful truths." One image, which as I shall try to show
significantly recurs in Swift's later work, sums up the point:
"Satire is a kind of glass, wherein beholders do generally discover everybody's face but their own; which is the chief reason
for that kind of reception it meets in the world, and that so very

few are offended with it." ("Preface of the Author," *Battle of the Books*.) Satire, then, has become an easy road to literary fame; evaluated not by its real influence on moral sensibility but by connoisseurs according to its rhetorical vehemence, its "lashes" on the world's insensitive posterior, it has become a kind of fascinating spectacle. But as a genuine force it has lost all effectiveness; it is but a barking dog. It even provides a perverse pleasure, not entirely unrelated to the erotic; and Swift could have added, if he had lived in our century, that it may provide an easy form of vicarious penance for guilt feeling. What, then, would be the greatest test of a satirist, or indeed of any conscientious wit? Not to sparkle more brilliantly than ever, not to show more ingenuity in devising images of denunciatory rhetoric, but to bring the message to readers' bosoms, to make men see themelves as well as their neighbors in the glass of satire. It would be oversimplifying, but with an element of truth, then, to say that the implied program involves moving from "literary" to "pragmatic" satire.

The strategy after the first volume may be described as one involving a spokesman of fixed position rather than the mercurial wit of *A Tale*. The result was loss of maneuverability: the viewpoint must remain unchanged, and the satirical objects must be maneuvered within range of the gun, which remains stationary. This procedure seems puzzling. Why should Swift have so deliberately restricted himself—indeed, why should he have eliminated the possibility of pure "wit" almost altogether? The answer, I would suggest, has to do with the self-imposed task of writing satire that for the first time is truly effective for the individual. It is through his spokesmen (not, as I shall try to show, always true *personae*) that Swift draws the reader into close relation with the satire, decreasing that detachment of the reader from the work which enables him to stand off and look on as a bystander at something that should involve him emotionally as well as intellectually and aesthetically. For the spokesman is in general a representative figure, a kind of Everyman from whom the reader cannot wholly detach himself. And to play this part, he cannot be that exceptional being, a wit.

Furthermore, the devices of the later satires involve the objectification, even the animation, of a satirical conceit which is in itself essentially simple. What might be simply a striking metaphor or paradox if presented in the course of an argument of satirical denunciation becomes far more powerful, even overwhelming, as it is expanded into a structure, perhaps a world of its own. The reader consequently finds himself within, rather than surveying from the outside, the satirical statement. To elucidate, I should like to examine from this standpoint what probably are Swift's three greatest satires after 1704.

An Argument to Prove That the Abolishing of Christianity in England May, as Things now Stand, Be Attended with Some Inconveniences, and Perhaps Not Produce Those Many Good Effects Proposed Thereby, said to have been written in 1708 (well in advance of the Sacheverell explosion), was directed, as is now generally agreed, at the conventional Church of England layman. The proposal in the title, so outrageous and so challenging to such a man, would instantly, strongly, capture attention. Who is presenting the Argument? The putative author (as one recent critic puts a very common opinion) is the unwitting victim of the satirical attack himself, for Swift

> . . . has constructed the figure of a nominal Christian, endowed him with a representative selection of mundane and materialistic values, depicted him as a servile defender of a lamentable status quo, and justified the appellation of 'Christian' only by providing his puppet with a shaky and superficial loyalty to the name of the Church.[6]

The whole question of *personae* in the major satires needs re-thinking. Certainly, Gulliver and the Drapier are fully depicted, independent characters—or at least developed enough to be clearly separable from their literary begetter. In the cases of *A Tale of a Tub*, the *Argument*, and *A Modest Proposal*, the situation is far less clear. Perhaps the problem is rather like that of "saving the appearances" of planetary movement; either the Ptolemaic or the Copernican system will do; but the latter, and its descendants, work much more simply and efficiently. So, it seems to me, the assumption of a true *persona* in these satires raises more difficulties, and obfuscates critical appreciation to a greater degree, than would the conception that through *personae* Swift is deliberately and openly speaking with an ironic voice. If we are to take the author of *An Argument* as a "nominal Christian," even a very nominal, mixed-up, shallow conformist, there is the difficulty to begin with of the statement that of course he regards the Gospel system, like other systems, as now "exploded." Surely we have to take this remark as ironic; and if one such irony can be attributed to the writer, why not others? Why is there not an intended ironic tone to the whole pamphlet? And it is well to remember that this satire appeared in the 1711 *Miscellanies*, which included such vitally important "straight" statements by Swift as *The Sentiments of a Church of England Man* and *The Dissentions between Nobles and Commons at Greece and Rome*; this volume is in fact Swift's credo, containing his most impressive efforts at statesmanlike reasoning about state and church. The bookseller, as if to avert the kind of theory I have quoted, emphatically asserts that we can take all the compositions in the book as being from the same hand.

It seems to me that careful reading of *An Argument* provides good reason to think it is deliberately, openly ironic. Indeed, at the end, Swift—as also in *A Modest Proposal*—drops any mask he has put on, with a sentence whose sardonic tone can hardly be mistaken. If the Gospel is extirpated,

> the Bank and East-India Stock may fall at least one *percent*.
> And since that is fifty times more than ever the wisdom of
> our age thought fit to venture for the *preservation* of Chris-
> tianity, there is no reason we should be at so great a loss,
> merely for the sake of *destroying* it.

The first of these sentences might be taken as compatible with a *persona* who is only a "servile defender of a lamentable status quo"; but the second statement destroys the illusion. The "thought fit" alone gives the whole thing away: the tone is very different from that of Gulliver in his encomiums of the Brobdingnagians, for example. And to assume that the author is only a "nominal Christian puppet" is to lose many wonderfully subtle ironic effects—the force of "without the least tincture," for example, in the following:

> . . . two young gentlemen of great hopes, bright wit, and
> profound judgment, who upon a thorough examination of
> causes and effects, and by the mere force of natural abilities,
> without the least tincture of learning, having made a dis-
> covery that there was no God. . . .

These and many other details help us realize what Swift meant when, in "Verses on the Death of Dr. Swift," he said of irony,

> Which I was born to introduce,
> Refin'd it first, and shew'd its use.

The meaning of this couplet, it seems to me, is that irony is a weapon which he had used, with great effect, as a deliberate device. The assumption that a *persona* who is no better than a solemn fool is the supposed author of this satire does violence to the "refin'd" technique of which Swift was so proud.

Finally, the restriction of *An Argument* to satire against hypo-

critical or lukewarm Christians greatly oversimplifies its real
scope. The work may be described as a device by which a
satirical conceit is used, like a searchlight, to illuminate one murky
group or faction after another, revealing the real motivations of
each. First, it should be remarked that the "proposal" itself—that
the abolition of Christianity would solve many of the most urgent
problems of the time—had some plausibility. Already the radical
deists and (although circumspectly) the third Earl of Shaftesbury
had intimated something like what was to be one great conviction of the Enlightenment—namely that revealed religion
has needlessly repressed and embroiled humanity, thereby causing
much of the evil in society. The situation in Swift's time might
have given at least superficial support to the proposition. The
question of the state church had set the whole nation into one
crisis after another, to the point where renewal of civil war
seemed not impossible. The passions aroused by the Toleration
Act and the controversy over the legitimacy of the rule of William
and Mary had split church and state both; and yet, in spite of
this fanatical quarreling over "religious principles," the real influence of religion on individual lives and on institutions was
plainly declining. Old people, the author remarks, remember
when religion was taken seriously. The church had become the
football in a wild game of opposing factions, and in 1709 the
egregious Sacheverell, with his inflammatory sermon on the Gunpowder Plot anniversary, was to bring the contest perilously close
to the explosion which for years had seemed almost inescapable.
It would not have taken a fool to argue that the abolition of a
church which was losing power over people's hearts and which
was causing so much civic turmoil might be wise. The author
applies the test of abolishing Christianity in turn to each party.
The larger issue is one that perennially divides social philosophers
and legislators. If such and such conditions are reformed, will
all discord cease and peace prevail? If people are quarreling like

cats and dogs, will they instantly cease when the apparent cause is removed? If there is discord over religion, will its removal end that battle? Swift emphatically belonged to the school which holds that the source of social conflict, as of social evil in general, is not external but internal: "Are party and faction rooted in men's hearts no deeper than phrases borrowed from religion, or founded upon no firmer principles?" Ironically, religion may even serve as an outlet for the portion of "enthusiasm" in the English nation, which otherwise could find even more dangerous forms of expression. But much of the quarrel is really directed "against religion in general; which, by laying restraints on human nature, is supposed the great enemy to the freedom of thought and action." Here as Swift acutely indicates, is the real heart of the matter. Should human nature be restrained, or liberated? Should thought and opinion be restricted in any degree? Will the ills of society be cured by removing the "restraints" and the religion behind them, which have misdirected the potential goodness of human beings? To show that human nature must have restraints and control, that social evils proceed from within the heart, was to be Swift's great undertaking, in *Gulliver IV*. Can we imagine a nominal, materialistic Christian writing these sentences?

It is worthy of note, also, that Swift's satire does not spare even the party with which he has often been identified—the zealous "high-flyers," the lower clergy who raised the cry "church in danger." To them he says: "Nor do I think it wholly groundless, or my fears altogether imaginary, that the abolishing of Christianity may perhaps bring the Church in danger, or at least put the senate to the trouble of another securing vote." He was aware that there could be a wide difference between crying "church in danger" and preserving true Christianity. Was it, indeed, the church or Christianity proper that was in danger? Fanatical "defense" of religion may be in its own way as damaging as the attack of an out-and-out enemy; it is a point in keeping with *A Tale of a Tub*. In summary, it seems to me that to visualize the writer of this satire as a hypocritical Christian, whether consciously or unconsciously, as a man dedicated to the interests of the City alone, is to raise a barrier between the reader and the work. The instrument of irony, skilfully and overtly used, enables Swift to examine and expose the whole situation *vis-à-vis* the church, the custodian of Christianity, under a revealing light, as straightforward argument could not.

The author of *A Modest Proposal for Preventing the Children of Poor People in Ireland from Being a Burden to Their Parents or Country, and for Making Them Beneficial to the Public* is, again, vaguely outlined. He is not the same as the Drapier, who is a separate personality. As I have intimated, the Drapier and Gulliver are the only two fully worked-up figures whom we can even describe, who are supposed to write any of Swift's major satires. And, it may be noted, the Drapier pamphlets are not unmixed satires. One reason for creating a fictitious author for these tracts against England's Irish policy was of course the necessity of giving Swift legal cover. But there is also the fact that in exposing the wrongs of economic policy, it was desirable to have as spokesman one who had, himself, substantially suffered from these measures, and one who could be considered an authority on such arcane problems of economics. A merchant might fit both parts; but anyone in the position of the man Swift on all scores would be inappropriate and unconvincing. Thus the author of *A Modest Proposal* remains little more than a voice. He begins, "It is a melancholy object to those who walk through this great town, or travel in the country. . . ." In Swift's day those most likely to come into contact with the poor and to travel through Ireland's poverty-stricken country were the clergy; and Swift, in his long clerical career, surely had seen more of the poor in both town and country than had most other of the higher clergy. I suggest that the author of *A Modest Proposal* may profitably be thought of as Swift himself, purposely adopting the ironic mode. At the end of this masterpiece of savage indignation, as too often we forget, the mask is dropped and a series of moderate and practical proposals for Irish self-help are described: they are in fact the real modest proposal.

Why, then, the horrific project, so soberly and mathematically worked out, which takes up most of the satire? As in *An Argument,* where Swift perhaps uses the shocker to illuminate and expose, so in *A Modest Proposal* he uses it quite literally as a form of shock treatment. Irony is the means for compelling his readers to see what is around them. After some crisis, people are sometimes heard to remark, "I seemed to see everything for the first time." The old patterns of perception have been broken up, the old assumptions about one's surroundings have disappeared. So with the proposal: the non-seeing, the complacent or despondent acceptance of things as they are is subjected to moral trauma. By extension, it has something like this effect on the modern reader; it seems to jar him into seeing anew his own world.

No mere presentation of the Irish plight, however eloquent, could have had such a result. As the project is expounded in all its horrifying but entirely appropriate detail, the reality becomes starkly plain. No other description of poverty, however vivid, has had a comparable effect. And this effect is made possible by the low-keyed, impersonal tone, neither invective nor denunciation. Swift had long since discovered that savage indignation is not most powerfully conveyed by savage vehemence. Against scolding, moral condemnation, calling down the wrath of heaven, the reader is well protected. It is the kind of thing for which the reader returns thanks, as Swift had observed so many years before. And most of all the reader is forearmed against anything that carries the stigma of "satire." On the other hand, the reader is denied the satisfying outlet of sentiment. What a novel Dickens could have made of the Irish situation! How many handkerchiefs would have been soaked with tears! But for those who read *A Modest Proposal* there is no such safety valve; nor is there the villainous scapegoat so indispensable to the sentimental novel—the evil person or persons who are the visible and vulnerable source of all that is wrong. Even England, which might have been blamed, is explicitly given but a secondary part. There is, then, no exciting and satisfying drama of oppressors and oppressed; the villains are universal greed, sloth, indifference. Swift's task is to make each guilty party—the aristocracy, merchants, clergy, lawyers, all the responsible classes—see himself in the mirror.

A major problem in analyzing and describing the genre of satire lies in its characteristic parasitism. Rather like a virus that invades and takes over a cell to support its own life, satire utilizes the various forms of literature for its own ends of rebuke and ridicule. We are all familiar with how the epic was thus utilized; with the way such forms as the scholastic oration were made to serve a purpose remote from their intended one; and of course satiric comedy has long been a tradition. But if satire takes on these varying forms, it works in a direction different from that of most literature. Schorer has remarked that "satire, which is essentially an art of oversimplification since it concentrates on a few if not only on a single characteristic, is inevitably in danger of overlooking the complexity of human nature." [7] But complexity as such is not the business of satire; the danger is that we shall expect from it, try to find in it, the kind of complexity appropriate to very different genres, and that what we expect may not be compatible with effective satirical writing. If satire presents a measured and meditative picture of life, it fails at least

in its ostensible purpose; indeed, satire is a last resort. Its bitter
medicine is required where the "constructive" has failed. Being
corrective, it tends to compensate excess with excess; if mild re-
proof and counsel could succeed, the satirist would have nothing
to do. So, at least, I believe Swift regarded his self-chosen function. Especially in the pragmatically successful satire at which
he aimed, we should be wary of highly complex discoveries in
content; variety and subtlety of effects are another matter. We
should, I now conclude, be wary of the almost theological
probing into the meaning of *Gulliver's Travels* in which several
of us have engaged; there is, at present, something like the
scholastic reading of Scriptural verses as types and allegories,
visible only to the initiated. It is ironic that Swift, who in *A
Tale of a Tub* ridiculed just this kind of subtlety, should have
become its object himself.

So, in sum, perhaps we should come back to the basic fact—
that *Gulliver's Travels* as a whole is the expansion, the massive
and gripping objectification, of some fundamentally simple
satiric conceits, which in fact can be summarized in a few short
statements. Johnson's famous comment on the first two Voyages
is in one way correct. Thinking "of big men and little men,"
even Johnson implied, required wit; but, certainly, he under-
estimated grossly in adding that then "it is very easy to do all the
rest." The opposition of bigness to pettiness itself is a brilliant
satirical image; but the success of the first two Voyages rests on
the way in which that conceit ceases to be merely a conceit and
becomes a world. A new kind of art was necessary to make this
rhetorical contrast opposition more than rhetoric, to make it
take hold of the reader's own experience as well as imagination.
The exposure of littleness, the consequence of intense ego-
centricity, is ingrained in every aspect of Lilliputian life and by
implication pointed up with immense effect by the opposing
world of Brobdingnagians. If Swift had written a verse satire

he could have stated directly the satiric contrast, and then have gone on to exemplify it with characters, as Pope did the abuse of riches. But no matter how masterfully Walpole, et al., might have been drawn, the reader would have remained external to the work. There would have been nothing like the feeling, which the common reader has had through the generations, of having been himself in Lilliput and Brobdingnag, of having lived within the satiric statement. Pope's satires are closely bound to their objects; Swift's masterpiece has reached untold millions of readers who never guessed that it had topical relevance. For, whatever one may think of the value of the *Travels,* it is most difficult to separate oneself from it, to view it at a distance.

In it, the reader vicariously experiences the episodes, as he himself experiences Gulliver's discoveries. Johnson acutely noted that *A Tale of a Tub* "exhibits a vehemence and rapidity of mind, a copiousness of images, and vivacity of diction, such as he afterwards never possessed, or never exerted." I think "never exerted" is correct; deliberately he forwent what must have been the delight of imaginative variety. After his first satires, he tended to utilize what might be called sub- or para-literary forms; in one sense, he left altogether the world of Literature as the neoclassical age knew it. *An Argument,* of course, is a pamphlet, a very common form of prose not usually identified with formal satire; in *A Modest Proposal* there is the sober and deadly benevolent Project. The use of the "scheme" for public improvement as vehicle is most disarming: could anyone be less inclined toward satire than the projector, with his dedicated zeal? Thus Swift overcame one major handicap of satirists; any hint of the sharpness, the "ill nature" of the satirist's touch in any work raises immediately a psychological defensiveness, if not antagonism, in the reader. Again, the proposal, shocking as it is to moral sensibility, is worked out with a care and foresight that set an example of the method that should be followed for more acceptable proposals such as those the author finally advances. Johnson remarked that Swift in his later work "pays no court to the passions," and employs very few metaphors. Superficially, this might seem to be strange procedure for a writer who is exposing a complex of evils and wrongs as gross as those of Ireland. But Swift must have been aware that the subject matter, brought directly into contact with the reader, would produce its own powerful response without any assistance from an intermediary, the author, and that that response is the more profound because the reader has not been instructed, so to speak, as to how he should respond. And, finally, the seemingly factual, unadorned narrative obviates any suspicion that the depiction is affected by that common failing of satire—hyperbolic treatment of the evils exposed; for most experienced readers of satire almost automatically discount in advance what the satirist is going to say.

Gulliver's Travels, as I have remarked, is one of the satires that utilize a non-literary or at best para-literary form: one, however, that had such popularity it was denounced by the third Earl of Shaftesbury as a prime cause of the rampant corruption of taste. Travelers' narratives were probably the most avidly read publications in the years just before *Gulliver,* as Defoe realized. But, I suspect, it was not to Defoe primarily, but to the originals that Swift went for the main features of his satirical vehicle. The travel narrative had the advantage, like other forms Swift employed, of being on the face far removed from satire; and its very popularity amply attested to its capacity for captivating the whole attention of the reader. The travel writer who most influenced Swift was Dampier, who is described as Gulliver's "cousin" and whom, Gulliver says, he advised to have his manuscript corrected by some young gentlemen at either university ("Letter to Sympson").

Even in the early days, Swift seems to have thought of the

possibilities opened up by Dampier's immensely popular book. For example, one of the treatises to be "speedily published" by the author of *A Tale of a Tub* is a "Voyage into England, by a Person of Quality in Terra Australis Incognita, translated from the Original." This proposal clearly was inspired by Dampier's description of the natives of this new world, who are, he says, the "miserablest People in the World . . . setting aside their Humane Shape, they differ but little from Brutes." [8] Here is the germ of the yahoo; but it appears that Swift originally thought of making them travelers into England, commentators perhaps like the exotic visitors who were to write satirical descriptions of England or other countries of Europe. But, it is instructive to note, *The Persian Letters, The Citizen of the World,* et al., have had a tiny fraction of the success of *Gulliver.* Probably even Swift would have had less effect had he used this strategy.

What, then, did he gain by sending his voyager to the exotic lands? First, there is the identification of the reader with the mariner. Gulliver, like Drapier, is a separate, straightforwardly established person, quite apart from Swift himself; and it is instructive to recall that it is these two putative authors who set their names to their compositions. Of the author of the *Argument* we know nothing, by explicit information; of the projector of *A Modest Proposal* we are told only the obviously ironic detail that "I have no children by which I can propose to get a single penny; the youngest being nine years old, and my wife past child-bearing." By contrast, the circumstances of Gulliver's family, education, career, are all entirely plausible, and combine to create a type of personality at the opposite pole from Swift's own. It is one with whom we can identify readily. The unmodulated but somehow graceful style of Dampier, his lack of idiosyncratic reactions, the sense of a kind of Everyman voyaging, encountering, objectively describing, could all be transferred to Gulliver; we trust what he says, partly because he seems to exhibit no special partisanship or ulterior motive in writing. When we have been cast ashore with Gulliver, we know not where, we are completely isolated from our familiar surroundings and must begin anew. So one perception is added to another to produce a total impression of the strange new land; it is rather like the process whereby, according to Lockean theory, the child acquires his ideas. This sense of discovery leads into a parable of civilization in its various aspects. After long and careful preparation—"softening up" the reader—Swift comes directly to the attack, with the comments of the king of Brobdingnag on conditions in England. By that time we have been disarmed, for satire seems remote. By that time, also, we have come to accept and to know this gigantic but human ruler. We have become acquainted with the king and queen in their domestic as well as public life, and we have seen them as truly benign and sensible rulers in their treatment of the tiny, terribly handicapped Gulliver. Unlike the superior, preachy and rather condescending inhabitants we usually find in Utopia, they are truly admirable in a human sense. When, therefore, the king rejects the use of gunpowder, and when he pronounces his verdict on the "most pernicious race of little odious vermin," we have forgotten that it is really Swift passing judgment on us, and we accept the heavy verdict as the considered opinion of a wise and impartial judge. So, with greatest skill, Swift has disarmed the antagonism, the natural resentment that should follow such a bitter condemnation.

Remembering the format of the *Travels,* moreover, helps place certain critical problems in perspective. For example, regret that the third Voyage lacks the unity evident in the others, and that it is not symmetrically contrasted with the fourth part as the first is to the second, arises from the expectation that the *Travels* should be in another form—that it should be a kind of formal satire. But Dampier and the other travelers conduct their narratives according to their wanderings; the author may devote several chapters to one area, in which he stayed for a considerable time, while he may touch several places in only a few pages. The restless movements of the third Voyage help to maintain the verisimilitude Swift desired. What is more significant about the third Voyage, however, is that it does not objectify one overarching satiric conceit. Instead there is (rare in Swift) a series of satirical descriptions. We miss the single, controlling center that we find in most of the later satires; but, as follies rather than vices are the subjects of this part, the sense of desultoriness, of rhetorical shapelessness, is appropriate. For great vices, even though they take many different shapes, are essentially few and are capable of precise definition; the demonstration, indeed, that they are the same under their disguises is an effective method of exposing them. How many and protean are the masks of pride, for example! But follies are innumerable and without controlling form: the swarming insects of the moral world.

But the end of this Voyage—the account of the struldbruggs —has another function, for it is the anteroom to the dark world of the yahoos. Up to this point in the work, the reader has a unique feeling of acceptance. We have gone with Gulliver through his dangerous and sometimes hilarious experiences and we have arrived at judgments arising from those experiences, but still only as spectators. We are still only partly involved in the satire. We feel our separation from Gulliver when he fusses about his reputation among the Lilliputians or when he cannot understand the king of Brobdingnag's strange attitude toward gunpowder. When he returns to his home, we can easily separate from him; we have been affected only as members of society. In our deep, individual existence, we are untouched. But the episode of the struldbruggs changes all that.

We are all mortals and would like to find compensation for the final indignity of life—the decay of the body—inescapable

                                                    unless
Soul clap its hands and sing, and louder sing
For every tatter in its mortal dress. . . .

As we "mature" (an instructive euphemism), we tell ourselves,
we grow wiser. Gulliver eagerly imagines that, with the struldbruggs, "I would mutually communicate our observations and
memorials through the course of time, remark the several grada-
tions by which corruption steals into the world, and oppose it
in every step, by giving perpetual warning and instruction to
mankind"; and so they "would probably prevent that continual
degeneracy of human nature so justly complained of in all ages."
Nowhere does Swift more openly expose his heart than here;
for the final purpose of all his work and life, he would certainly
have said, was to resist that cyclical movement of degeneration
which he and Pope and many others thought the great menace
to civilization. The yahoos will appear as the awful evidence of
what "continual degeneracy of human nature" means. How
wonderful then, if by advancing age men could learn, through
experience and constant growth of wisdom, to preserve all that
is valuable in life forever! Shaw, in *Back to Methuselah,* advances (without a grain of satire) the faith in salvation through
longevity. Alas, even this dream is dissipated as we contemplate
the struldbruggs in their obscene senility. Gulliver is told by his
interpreter that he had fallen into a few mistakes "through the
common imbecility of human nature, and upon that allowance
was less answerable for them." So we have begun our initiation
into the satire upon man; we have begun to sense that the corruption of human nature is something that is in each of us as
individuals as well as in the abstraction called the human species.
We begin to see ourselves as members of the human race, who
cannot escape from evil, and not simply as Englishmen, or as
civilized persons who have conquered bestial tendencies.

It is of course the last Voyage that has been most responsible for the Swift legend, for the mixture of admiration, fear, and hatred with which Swift's name is associated. The hysterical reactions to the yahoos have perhaps no counterpart among responses to any other literary work. There was some consolation in the once widely believed notion that what Sir Edmund Gosse called "the awful satire of the Yahoos" was the "horrible satisfaction of disease," the product of "a brain not wholly under control." Thackeray's *cri de coeur* against the yahoos suggests that, whether Swift's intellect was under control or not, Thackeray's own was not in perfect order. "What had this man done? What secret remorse was rankling at his heart, what fever was boiling in him, that he should see all the world blood-shot?" Yet Swift could have retorted that *Vanity Fair,* even its title, gives support to his own picture of the degeneracy of human nature. The shrillness of these outbursts, even from writers as normally placid as Sir Walter Scott, suggests that the satire has touched them in a special way. Swift has forced them to see what appears to be their own image, but horribly distorted in the mirror: they look for any means of escape from that vision, for a mirror reflects the truth. Swift might well have taken the attacks, even in his own time, as the best proof that he had indeed accomplished the seemingly impossible—to make the world really feel the lash of satire. Pope called Swift an "Avenging Angel of wrath," and asserted that he would make the "wretched pityful creatures of this world" "*Eat your Book,* which you have made as bitter a pill for them as possible"; it was indeed Swift's achievement to realize this, the ancient goal of strong satire.

Yet, remarkably, the last Voyage, so far as its abstractly stated "message" goes, says nothing either new or unique. Its point is that of many critiques which discover a congenital and power-

ful strain of destructiveness and pride in the animal man. John
Wesley asserted that "If . . . we take away this foundation, that
man is by nature foolish and sinful, fallen short of the glorious
image of God, the Christian system falls at once; nor will it
deserve so honourable an appellation, as that of 'a cunningly
devised fable.' " [9] He composed many treatises and sermons in
defense of the doctrine of original sin, against the increasingly
optimistic views that burgeoned as the century went on. Over
and over he repeated what might be called the archetypal expression of the old attitude:

> Are there any of the brutal kind that do not more regularly
> answer the design of their creation? Are there any brutes
> that we ever find acting so much below their original char-
> acter, . . . as mankind does all over the earth? Were this
> globe of earth to be surveyed from one end to the other, by
> some spirit of a superior order, it would be found such a
> theatre of folly and madness, such a maze of mingled vice
> and misery, as would move the compassion of his refined
> nature to a painful degree.[10]

Such outcries may shock us somewhat, but not deeply. Satires in
which beings from a more advanced world survey with indignation and pity the "theatre of folly and madness" are not un-
common; none has evoked a tithe of the passion that Swift's
fable of the yahoos has aroused. Yet Wesley himself suggested
a comparative evaluation of mankind that, one might think,
would be even more offensive to our pride of species than Swift's:

> . . . every man is conscious to himself, that in this respect
> he is by nature a very beast. Sensual appetites, even those of
> the lowest kind, have, more or less, the dominance over
> him. They lead him captive; they drag him to and fro, in
> spite of his boasted reason. The man, with all his good-
> breeding and other accomplishments, has no pre-eminence

over the goat; nay, it is much to be doubted, whether the beast has not the pre-eminence over him.[11]

As if to demonstrate the identification of Swift's position with the traditional Christian belief, he cites Gulliver's conversations with the Houyhnhnm master about the English nation as proof of the degenerate condition of men in even their "most enlightened state—Protestantism." And he adds, impatiently, apparently quoting (inaccurately) from memory the final page of *Gulliver's Travels*:

. . . meanwhile we gravely talk of the *Dignity of our Nature*, in its present state! This is really surprising, and might easily drive even a well-tempered man to say, 'One might bear with men if they would be content with those vices and follies to which nature has entitled them. . . .'

John Wesley is renowned as a "well-tempered" man, and certainly has never been accused of misanthropy. This fact alone demonstrates how far from unique or neurotic were Swift's views. The connection between traditional satire, sermonizing, and theology had long been close; and Christian symbols of sin were incorporated into the yahoo image. Yet the tradition of *Gulliver IV* derives mainly from the literary side. Here it is important to realize that the fable of the yahoos and houyhnhnms, which seems to stand by itself as the singular product of an untypical mind, is only one of a sub-genre of satires on human nature. And it is the culmination, the imaginative realization of that line, much as *Paradise Lost* rests on and is the culmination of a series of now forgotten versifications of Scriptural narrative. We remember Swift, as we remember Milton, because both uniquely succeeded in doing what many had essayed. The satire on man sought to bring home to the individual in his inner being, to make him recognize in his own identity the reality of the abstract proposition that evil is ingrained in the nature of man. It is not only the theoretical point that is at issue: nothing was easier for a conventional and sincere church-man than to assent to the teaching in the catechism; nothing was harder than to make him see the old Adam in himself as well as in "vous autres." It is likely that most church-goers, re-citing the general confession, have a comfortable feeling that any personal faults (surely not too large) have been taken care of. Sermons like Wesley's were intended to bring home the reality of the great doctrine to each person. Likewise, readers of the "satires upon man" could accept the rhetorical strictures without feeling much personal uneasiness.

One of the most respected examples of the satire on mankind is Boileau's *Satire VIII*. Its thesis sets forth the whole essential of the yahoo-houyhnhnm opposition.

> De tous les animaux qui s'élevent dans l'air,
> Qui marchent sur la terre, ou nagent dans la mer,
> Paris au Perous, du Japon jusqu'à Rome,
> Le plus sot animal, à mon avis, c'est l'homme.
> Quoi? dira-t-on d'abord, un ver, une fourmi,
> Un insecte rampant qui ne vit qu'à demi,
> Un taureau qui rumine, une chèvre qui broute,
> Ont l'esprit mieux tourné que n'a l'homme. Oui, sans doute.[12]

The piece is a dialogue, resembling such "epistles" as Pope's "Prologue to the Satires." The part of human nature is taken by a Sorbonne doctor nicknamed appropriately "la machoire d'âne"—the poem ends with an ass observing mankind who, having been given power of speech, concludes, "l'homme n'est qu'une bête." The doctor gives conventional defensive argu-ments for man's rationality and his exalted position in the earthly creation. These points are granted, but man's actual behavior becomes the more culpable because of them: he is merely "le plus sot." By comparison, here is the verdict of the houyhnhnm master: "But when a creature pretending to reason could be capable of such enormities, he dreaded lest the corruption of that faculty might be worse than brutality itself." The old rhetorical conceits have, as it were, come to life, and, in a monstrous waking nightmare, come to take us. Not even Rochester, easily the most powerful of Swift's predecessors, achieved this effect. An instructive contrast between mere rhetorical statement and inclusive satire may be seen by quotation from Robert Gould's "A Satyr upon Man" (1689); it in fact is as vehement as Swift's, but how much less affecting!

> Man! who was made to govern all things, yet
> No other Brute is govern'd with so little wit:
> So oddly temper'd and so apt to stray,
> There's not a Dog but's wiser in his way:

The force of "other Brute" is lost on us; it reaches us only when we see the yahoo brutes. And in the Prologue to his *Satyrs and Epistles* Gould makes no apology for the bitterness of his book:

> Mankind is criminal, their Acts, their Thoughts;
> 'Tis Charity to tell them of their fau'ts.

Could Swift have said more?

For the satirists in the strong tradition, the satire upon mankind was far more than a literary exercise. It was in fact the capstone, the guarantee of the validity of the satirical medicine. The satirist has always been in a peculiarly uncomfortable position among his fellow authors. He must prove, to himself as much as to others, that he is not motivated by a perverse desire to wound, or driven by morbid resentment against the world for its neglect of him. He must demonstrate, too, that the "ill-nature" of sharp satire does not cause harm rather than good. The responsible satirist must in some degree be a "misanthrope," but, in the famous phrase Swift used in his letter to Pope (September 1725) "not in Timon's manner": he must neither write out of personal pique and disillusionment, nor sulkily reject humanity. It is necessary, therefore, to show that the discipline of ridicule and admonition is required by the deep-rooted character of human follies and vices; education, positive instruction, and example are just not enough.

The problem of justifying satire from the essential make-up of human beings had by Swift's time taken on a new urgency. Wesley, in a passage quoted above, expressed his indignation about "talk of the *Dignity of our Nature.*" The old phrase had become the banner, as it were, of an insurgent force in the Western tradition. Shaftesbury had advanced the revolutionary proposition that a human being is equipped by nature to play his proper and successful part in the great system, and that if he fails to do so it is because bad training, bad government, and perverted religious opinions have twisted and dwarfed him. Thus the fault, according to this doctrine, is not in ourselves but in our world: correct that and liberated human nature will be what it was meant to be. Some of the most influential writers of the time had cast doubt on the traditional view of man. Both Steele and Addison, although formally acknowledging some degree of degeneration, had in fact undermined the whole conception on which traditional satire and sermon alike had been based. Steele enthusiastically exclaimed: "There is nothing I contemplate with greater pleasure than the dignity of human nature, which often shows itself in all conditions of life" (*Tatler* 86). True, the glorious building is a ruin, but one that plainly reveals the nobility of its plan; and it can be repaired and restored to its "ancient symmetry and beauty." The thrust of this metaphor is significant. Human nature, like a physical structure, can be repaired step by step, each improvement permanently making good some dilapidation. By contrast, Swift's orthodox opinion might be called biological, emphasizing the continuity of heredity and the repetition in each generation of transmitted patterns of behavior. There is no guarantee, indeed no prospect at all, that repairs by one generation will persist through succeeding ones.

The "innate sinfulness of man" might be compared to a hereditary disease from which all suffer. In some persons it may be arrested but it can never be cured. It would be the height of pride for anyone, even an Arbuthnot, to think that in him the affliction has been entirely and permanently eliminated. This point needs to be understood to appreciate why Swift saw the yahoo in all mankind. Steele, in accordance with his pleasure in contemplating the natural dignity of humanity, implies that not the lash of the satirist or the harsh sermonizer, but "a happy education, conversation with the finest spirits, looking abroad into the works of nature" and like positive measures are the appropriate ways to repair the ruin. A few weeks later, Addison took up the same subject. He remarks that a show of acrobats, who twisted themselves into all manner of unnatural positions, disgusted him, for "I must confess, there is nothing that more pleases me in all that I read in books, or see among mankind, than such passages as represent human nature in its proper dignity" (*Tatler* 108).

One of Addison's observations must have affected Swift poignantly. The best of the ancients, Addison remarks, accentuate the positive and "cultivate man's natural grandeur of soul, hopes of immortality and perfection, etc." It is the moderns who "depreciate human nature, and consider it under its worst appearances." Leading the moderns are "our modish French authors, or those of our own country who are imitators and admirers of that trifling nation," sniffed the true-born Tatler. They "endeavour to make no distinction between man and man, or between the species of man and that of brutes." At the nadir is the "celebrated Rochefoucault," "the great philosopher for administering of consolation to the idle, the envious, and worthless part of mankind." All this must have seemed as a gauntlet thrown down to the author of *The Battle of the Books*. The yahoo-brute seems almost a direct response; and Swift appears to have taken up the gauntlet, many years later, when he took as epigraph for "Verses on the Death of Dr. Swift" one of Rochefoucauld's most notorious aphorisms.

> As Rochefoucault his maxims drew
> From nature, I believe 'em true:
> They argue no corrupted mind
> In him; the fault is in mankind.

What is unique about the last Voyage, then, is not its message and not its "misanthropy." Swift, as his "straight" writing shows, was a witty, relatively conventional moralist and theologian who pretended to no strikingly original philosophical and moral opinions; his ideas about human nature and society and government followed pretty much in conservative, although not extreme, lines. Most misleading is the lingering notion that Swift somehow was not in control of his creative work, that passion spontaneously overflowed and guided the pen, or that it interfered with the execution of the plan. The perfection and consistency of the details of the later satires, which even Swift's most censorious critics have acknowledged, is inconsistent with a shaping mind unbalanced by passion or conflict.

In the last Voyage, therefore, I suggest that Swift finally succeeded in achieving that goal intimated in the first volume of satires—to force the reader to include himself in the satiric reflection. There is a series of passages which seem to recall the metaphor of satire as a kind of glass, which I quoted above. First, in Brobdingnag:

> Neither indeed could I forbear smiling at my self, when the Queen used to place me upon her hand towards a looking-glass by which both our persons appeared before me in

full view together; and there could nothing be more ridiculous than the comparison: so that I really began to imagine my self dwindled many degrees below my usual size. (II, 3)

This episode occurs after the scholars of Brobdingnag have decided he is only a *lusus naturae,* and just before the account of the knavish behavior of the Queen's dwarf—both sufficiently mortifying. Yet Gulliver can now smile at his relatively tiny, ludicrous appearance: satire has performed some of its compensatory correction of pride. Far more bitter are passages in *Gulliver IV* having to do with reflections. The master "seemed confident, that instead of reason, we were only possessed of some quality fitted to increase our natural vices; as the reflection from a troubled stream returns the image of an ill-shapen body, not only *larger* but more *distorted*" (IV, 5). The full shock of self-recognition occurs toward the end of his stay: "When I happened to behold the reflection of my own form in a lake or fountain, I turned away my face in horror and detestation of myself, and could better endure the sight of a common yahoo, than of my own person" (IV, 10). And our last glimpse of Gulliver is in England, where he is accustoming himself to "behold my figure often in a glass, and thus if possible habituate myself by time to tolerate the sight of a human creature."

It has been suggested that Swift "may not have foreseen what would happen when, in the Fourth Part, he involved Gulliver for the first time in situations which, though intended to represent abstract issues, were actually such as to provoke intense emotional participation, rather than cool and rational observation, in his readers. For the same reason Swift may not have seen how his erstwhile persona had become a character, and thus lost the element of distance from the reader, which is so essential to the *persona's* ironic function. . . ." [13] This is indeed what happens, but I doubt that it came about through inadvertence or miscalculation; indeed, I would suggest, it is precisely "cool and rational observation," the separation of the reader from the satire, that Swift wanted to avert: for he wanted to advance satire on man from its usual state, from "abstract issues" to an experience very similar to that of the reader himself. Nor, I suggest, is *Gulliver* as a whole, and this Voyage in particular, predominantly ironic in effect. The technique is different from that of *An Argument* and the *Modest Proposal,* where irony is employed to produce the effects desired. (This is of course not to deny that there are ironic, as it were, sub-effects to the large prevailing satiric conceits.)

Gulliver's continuing aversion to his human fellows after his return, despite his kind treatment by strangers as well as his own family, is necessary to prevent the reader from seizing an opportunity to escape from the grip of the satirical engine. Were Gulliver to moderate his insight, to attain that "balanced" view which would seem to be wisdom, the reader would instantly see an exit. Why of course, he would say, there are many disguised yahoos among us, to be sure; how dreadful, and how praiseworthy of Swift to show *them* what *they* really are. And so his image would disappear from the satirical glass, and he would look upon, not from within the satire. But Swift's strategy of totally involving the reader in the satire, however effective in terms of brute psychological force, does certainly raise difficult problems of evaluation. The uncompromising ending, with its almost nihilistic negation of the "dignity of man," seems to leave us stranded in a spiritual waste land—even though, to be sure, it is with satire and not tragedy we are dealing. The ludicrous complaints of Gulliver's "Letter to Sympson," however, may have been intended to reduce the level of the effect, and conceivably, it might even be compared to the "after-piece" of the theatrical performance of tragedy in the age.

The houyhnhnms, it has been said, have all the virtue and the yahoos all the life. The fact is not accidental. For, if we take this whole Part as the objectification of the satiric conceit of contrasting men and animals as if they had men's advantages (which we have seen to have been traditional), the houyhnhnms are there, not to set literal examples, but to complete the comparison. The houyhnhnms are in reality collections of anti-vices. Because deceitfulness is a common failing of men, the houyhnhnms are incapable of saying the thing that is not; because selfishness and indifference are characteristic human traits, the houyhnhnms are perfectly benevolent. None of these goods can be described as virtues in the true sense; they are natural endowments, counters to demonstrate human faults. The point is that only man, with his flawed "lower" nature, is constantly confronted by an option; he must overcome himself to use his faculty of reason. This point is the epitome of the ancient doctrine of original sin.

In brief summary, my message is that Swift's importance is narrow but deep; it lies in his mastery of his particular kind of art, of its technique in relation to his intentions, not in the special complexity and originality of his insight into the depths of human nature; and so it is by examining that art, its ends and means, that we come to comprehend rightly Swift's greatness.

Afterword

Malvin R. Zirker, Jr.

INDIANA UNIVERSITY

Malcolm Bradbury's *Stepping Westward,* a novel set in part at least at Indiana University, where Mr. Bradbury once taught freshman composition, contains a classroom scene in which the hero, James Walker, encounters problems familiar to any one who has taught *A Modest Proposal* to freshmen. In response to his request for opinions on Swift's cure for Ireland's ills, one young lady volunteers her doubt that "even under any circumstances people should eat children," though, eagerly tolerant, she adds, "I guess there's another point of view, but I don't think I'd agree with it." Walker's trials continue:

> "That's a very humane view, Miss Lindstrom," said Walker, "but why don't you think people should eat children?"
>
> Miss Lindstrom looked at Walker with bright blue eyes. "Are you really in favour of eating children, Mr. Walker? Are you *really?*"
>
> "Not really," said Walker. "Was Swift?"
>
> "Was who?" said Miss Lindstrom.
>
> "Was Swift? Jonathan Swift who wrote the essay I asked you to read."

"Well, I guess he must have been," said Miss Lindstrom.
"He wouldn't have said he was if he wasn't, would he?"

Walker . . . noticed that, at the front of the classroom,
Jabolonski was sitting straining, with outstretched hand. At
Walker's glance he said, "I think the guy was kidding."
   Miss Lindstrom looked at Mr. Jabolonski. "Why would
he be kidding?" she asked. "What would he kid about a
thing like that for?"
   "Well, duh, I dunno, but maybe he was tryin' to get
sumpn done about all dat famine and all."

The direction of *A Modest Proposal* perhaps having been
sufficiently adumbrated, Mr. Walker now feels it time to focus
on artistic process: "'What's the name for that kind of literary
procedure?' Walker asked. Mr. Jabolonski ducked his head and
scratched it with a large hand; after a moment he said, 'Duh,
I dunno, lyin'?'"
   More professional discussions of Swift and of satire have at
times proceeded with equal indirection, and the mystery of
Swift's presence or absence in a literary mode frequently identified more opprobriously than that merely of the lie direct has
puzzled clearer heads than Miss Lindstrom's. It is at least amus-
ing to note how even this brief humorous (and satiric) discussion of satire touches on subjects that continue to puzzle: the
direction of the satiric attack and its reference to an outside
world, the intentions and personality of the satirist, and the literary status of his work.
   Happily, the three essays here printed were only briefly, and
in turn, the last word on a subject we may continue to consider.
Though each essay focuses, generally speaking, on a single
satirist and, with Mr. Rosenblum and Mr. Tuveson, on a single
satiric work, all three papers inevitably consider the larger and
recurrent questions inherent in their subject. They are thus valu-

able not only for their local insights but for their illustration and clarification of topics central to any consideration of satire. All three writers, for instance, are sharply aware of the difficulties surrounding definitions of satire, an awareness that establishes one of the points of identity these in other ways disparate papers share. "If there has been published any meaningful discussion of that essence shared by Donne's second satire, the second voyage of *Gulliver's Travels,* and the second act of *The Beggars' Opera,*" Mr. Miner writes, "I confess my ignorance of it." The "protean form" of satire, in Mr. Miner's phrase, the "bastard form" in Mr. Rosenblum's, and Mr. Tuveson's observation about satire's "characteristic parasitism" that "rather like a virus . . . invades and takes over a cell to support its own life," all remind us that satire knows not whether it prefers a substantival or adjectival existence and that all too readily it encourages a Polonius-like multiplicity of categories. Though not new, questions such as these observations imply about the nature of satire remain lively, for they ask whether or not satire has a center, an essential life of its own, a way of being that truly distinguishes it from other literary modes.

In chapter fourteen of *Martinus Scriblerus. Peri Bathous: or, of the Art of Sinking in Poetry,* Pope had ironically connected "Dedications, Panegyrics, or Satires" as similar literary modes, all governed chiefly by the *"Golden Rule* of *Transformation"* whereby vices or virtues are converted into their bordering counterparts. Success in this activity primarily indigenous to Grubstreet is dependent largely on judicious recourse to "our *Rhetorical Cabinet,"* where one may find "a full collection of Topics and Epithets to be used in the Praise and Dispraise of Ministerial and Unministerial Persons." It is precisely this mechanical and lifeless view of satire that each of these essays, in its own way, rejects; and their common insistence that, despite its apparent parasitism, satire has its own natural rhetoric establishes a larger shared bond between them.

Interestingly, Mr. Miner and Mr. Rosenblum both seriously make Pope's ironic connection between satire and panegyric, and Mr. Tuveson too notes the connection that already existed for Pope and Swift between panegyric and satire. Mr. Miner, arguing that "we may represent the central concern of satire in the process of the ruin of an ideal city," observes that the "polar opposite of this process is the raising by panegyric of 'the enduring monument,' the conferring of an immortality immune to time the devourer of things, as Ovid suggests." Mr. Rosenblum points out that the same method Pope had used in the *Temple of Fame* to celebrate those names which "From Time's first Birth, with Time it self shall last: / These ever new, nor subject to Decays, / Spread, and grow brighter with the Length of Days" could be used in *The Dunciad* to "celebrate those whose names were already forgotten." But the process of transformation whereby the satiric artifact is created is not arbitrary or mechanical. Mr. Miner reminds us that "the greatest English satirists wear singing-robes as many-colored as Joseph's coat," and the image of the satirist's song is cited by Mr. Rosenblum as well.

In arguing for a "natural rhetorick" of satire these papers center on the major critical focus of recent writings on the subject. To describe satire's customary rhetorical strategies, and thereby illuminate its special literary way of being, has been the essential purpose of the work of both Paulson and Kernan, for example.[1] Perhaps not as obviously central but still recurrent have been questions concerning the satirist's personality and the presence or absence of a *persona* in works of satire. Both Mr. Rosenblum and Mr. Tuveson allude to the traditional view of the satirist as a man "motivated by a perverse desire to wound or by morbid resentment against the world for its neglect of him," as a "man with a bias, in some striking cases literally thrown off balance by curvature of the spine, a clubfoot, or affliction of the middle ear." That nervous attempts to disarm the satirist of his power to speak tellingly are not quite out of fashion is suggested by the forty tables printed in W. A. Pannenborg's *Écrivains Satiriques: Caractère et Tempérament* (Presses Universitaires de France, Paris, 1955), a study which attempts to classify satirists by personality types. Among other findings, Dr. Pannenborg discovers that satirists are extreme egotists and that while only 36 per cent of ordinary mortals are vain and only 47 per cent are proud, the figures for satirists are 71 and 86 per cent respectively.[2]

The pervasive influence of Maynard Mack's essay, "The Muse of Satire,"[3] in establishing the concept of satirist as rhetor, as one who creates a voice and perhaps a personality for strategic purposes in his work, would seem to provide a way to answer that long line of readers who, with Dr. Pannenborg, seek to reject the satirist's challenge by exposing the dark and uncontrolled forces of his personality. More satisfying for many than the possible biographical defenses has been the argument that the voice one hears in satire is a made thing, the product of art not life. Kernan, for example, writes that the public character of the satirist is "a function of satire itself, and not primarily an attribute of the man who writes the satire." Thus "the typical satirist . . . is brought into being by the necessities of satire. If the attack on vice is to be effective, the character who delivers it must appear the moral opposite of the world he condemns; he must be fervent, he must be horrified at what he sees, and he must be able to distinguish between vice and virtue without any philosophical shillyshallying about 'what is right and what is wrong?' The traditional character of the satirist enables him to perform each of these acts."[4]

The concept of the *persona*, then, rescues satire both from the biographer and from the offended spokesman for life's smiling pleasantries, and places it clearly in the artistic fields of light illuminated by literary tradition. It is most important to note, however, the recurrence of doubt, primarily in Mr. Tuveson's essay, concerning the validity of our concept of the *persona*. One notes the discouraging multiplicity of voices that echo in the chambers of the mind of the twentieth-century reader. Mr. Booth advises us of at least three creators of *Tom Jones*: the narrator who addresses us directly, the implied author who both creates and is created by him, and the biographical Fielding himself, who is rather off stage and presumably silent about his merely quotidien self. If we follow Mr. Holland, however, there is another voice in the cellarage who communes silently with us past and by means of his heaped up defenses. The writer, unlike Mistress Quickly, certainly cannot exclaim "any man knows where to have me."

In the Alexander Lectures in English delivered at the University of Toronto in 1959, Bertrand Bronson, speaking of an earlier satirist and ironist, bravely observed, "It is a current fashion, not to say a fad, to discuss *persona* in works of fiction, and of late there has been a rash of talk about Chaucer's *persona,* meaning the 'I' in his poetry. I have little hesitation in saying that nine-tenths of this talk is misguided and palpably wrong."[5] It is wrong, he argues, because Chaucer wrote for oral delivery and the concept of the *persona* makes sense only in the world of print. In the course of his argument, however, he comments on how the complexities of conversational tones do not create a variety of *personae* but reflect the potential pleasures of civilized social intercourse and contain the "silent process" of irony:

> Nobody supposes that when a man talks about himself in a social environment, in a company met to enjoy one another, he need treat what he says as a deposition in a court of law. If he is humorous, wise, and witty, he will be self-conscious in varying degree; and he will try to be modest and un-

assuming, entertaining, and probably ironic in the way he
expresses himself. . . . If he is given to irony, he will add
spice to his discourse. Everyone knows how much the pleasure of conversation is enhanced by such continuous play of
mind; and self-mockery, or the refusal to take oneself too
seriously, is an essential ingredient in personal allusions if
they are not to become offensive. It misleads no one: the
audience neither takes the speaker at his literal word nor
jumps to the conclusion that the discrepancy between what
it hears and what it sees and knows signifies that someone
else is being talked about. The remarks, indeed, gain their
effect by virtue of the fact that all the while a tacit comparison with another image is proceeding. This silent process
is the very core of irony.[6]

That Mr. Bronson's scepticism toward Chaucerian *personae*
can be extended to those of the Augustan satirists is fully demonstrated in Mr. Ehrenpreis's essay "Personae." [7] Ehrenpreis too
proceeds from a strong sense of the complexities of "self" in life
as well as literature, and points out that "if we abandoned the
postulate of an essence distinct from all its manifestations," that
is, the notion of a single "real self," we would recognize what has
always been obvious: "We cannot think or even dream without
'posing.' As long as a man's character is alive, it is trying out
roles in language, in conduct. At the same time, although one
'self' does continually displace another, each remains a form or
mode of revelation of the real person." [8] Ehrenpreis's movement
from this commonsensical psychological observation to its application to literature is part of a complex argument not to be
reproduced here. Among his conclusions, however, is that if,
in a poem like *An Epistle to Dr. Arbuthnot,* we allow "the
separation of the speaker from the author,"

the connection of the poem with history is destroyed. . . . if
such an approach is valid, Pope has been inept, because the

speaker of the *Epistle* appeals continuously to history, resting his defense upon the verifiable truth of his data. Now this appeal seems to me anterior to the surface of rhetorical persuasion. If the author of this poem were not the great poet of his age, if his relations with his parents were not well known to have been as he testifies, if Atticus and Sporus did not belong to public life, the force of the poem would dwindle.[9]

Though not rejecting the notion of the *persona* entirely and rather wishing to indicate those instances in which the presence of an "ironical persona" can usefully be described, the drift of Ehrenpreis's argument is clear and is clearly stated in his concluding observations:

> In didactic or lyric poetry, as in the reflective or polemical essay, the author must be regarded as the speaker. He may talk ironically; he may imitate a man he despises; he may ask you to sneer at the fool he is copying; he may in mockery talk like his foolish audience. But unless we treat the material as indicating, however indirectly, what the author believes and is, we do not discover the meaning of the work; and if we miss its meaning, we cannot judge its form.[10]

As I mentioned earlier, Mr. Tuveson has his doubts about *personae* too. Whether in *A Modest Proposal*, for example, one hears the voice of Swift or that of a created character may be a problem, he suggests, "rather like that of 'saving the appearances' of the planetary movement; either the Ptolemaic or the Copernican system will do," but he goes on to say that "the assumption of a true *persona* in these satires raises more difficulties, and obfuscates critical appreciation to a greater degree, than would the conception that through *personae* Swift is deliberately and openly speaking with an ironic voice." His discussion of *An Argument to Prove That the Abolishing of Christianity in England May, as Things now Stand, Be At-*

tended with Some Inconveniences, and Perhaps Not Produce those Many Good Effects Proposed Thereby that follows makes it clear that it is not a minor point about rhetorical deployment that is at stake in asking whether it is Swift or a "nominal, materialistic Christian" who is the "voice" of *An Argument*.

I have called attention at such length to some of the issues surrounding the concept of the *persona* because this opens, it seems to me, a problem central to all satire, to say the least, and points up the most critical area of connection, if not of agreement, between the three essays here printed. That is, questions about the *persona*, as Mr. Ehrenpreis's essay makes perfectly clear, are ultimately related to questions concerning the satiric work's relationship to the (or is it "a"?) real world. What is the relation of the satiric vision to that world? Is satire essentially an attack upon "discernible historic particulars"? Is it in any sense mimetic? Is the satirist a rhetorician intent on persuading, or is he an artist, contemplatively creative? Is the end of satire moral reformation or esthetic pleasure? These are the major questions directly or indirectly asked in these essays and they are variously answered.

These issues are joined most directly by Mr. Tuveson and Mr. Rosenblum. The latter wittily rejects the notion that satire is primarily a kinetic art form that has as its end a palpable alteration of the real world. If this were true would not the satiric work be a fleetingly existent middle term between the writer's moral intention and the hopefully salutary consequences of his satiric act? Satire, if its end is moral reformation, perhaps is justified only in its effect and without a discernible effect remains merely a rhetorical act full of sound and fury. If, moreover, one attempts to read a work such as *The Dunciad* in light of its references to historical particulars he encounters a bewildering display of imaginative alteration of fact. *The Dunciad* is scarcely an act of historical mimesis. Rather, "the dunces are mute and passive, completely subject to the 'design' of the poet," and the real center of the poem is not an ethically based attack on the forces of dullness but an artistic response to the question "how may the deeds of dullness be converted into an act of wit?"

Mr. Tuveson, on the other hand, argues that the greatest satires "work," that they oblige the reader to look at himself in the satiric glass. *A Tale of a Tub,* rather like Mr. Rosenblum's *Dunciad,* exhibits an endlessly varied wit and "although it might have some influence on the general climate of opinion, making informed readers more sensitive to frauds and follies in religion and philosophy, its main function seems to be to delight the rational imagination with its dazzling display." But in *Gulliver's Travels,* by means of an art that largely conceals itself, Swift forces us into involvement and response. *Gulliver's Travels* effects, if not social or moral alterations in society, a response in its readers that cannot be described as merely esthetic but rather is connected with our ethical life.

Mr. Tuveson suggests that we may trace a movement in Swift's satire from literary to pragmatic satire, from the dazzling display of wit in the *Tale of a Tub* that delights the reader but leaves him unreformed and uninvolved to the relatively bare but highly kinetic and affective satire of *A Modest Proposal* and *Gulliver's Travels.* This distinction is not unrelated to that which Mr. Rosenblum cites from Northrop Frye between "ornamental speech" and "persuasive speech": "ornamental rhetoric acts on its hearers statically, leading them to admire its own beauty or wit; persuasive rhetoric tries to lead them kinetically toward a course of action." This suggests of course that perhaps the most appropriate critical response to a work of satire is dependent on whether or not that work best fits in the category of literary or pragmatic satire, whether its rhetoric can best be understood as ornamental or persuasive. Thus for some works one properly adorns himself in what Mr. Rosenblum terms "the formalist's velvet jacket," for others he should be more sternly attired in the "moralist's toga."

In a recent article in *Genre* (I [1968], 13) Patricia Meyer Spacks fairly observes that "efforts to isolate the nature of satire have fallen historically into two general categories, emphasizing either purpose or technique." If this statement correctly describes the poles of criticism of satire, as I believe it does, one can also argue that it is difficult to imagine a convincing criticism of satire that restricts itself to the confines of either extreme. Mr. Miner, for instance, rejects a purely mimetic theory of art in favor of "a transformational view of literature" which allows us to emphasize "the process of creation," and which, for satire, centers on the artistic means whereby the satirist creates "a vision of man, the state, arts, or the world degenerating before one's eyes." Yet though a successful work of satire creates an internally coherent moral world to which our major attention should perhaps be given, he does not ignore our inevitable need "to be reasonably sure that 'a better or worse likeness' is being taken." It is impossible, he suggests, "to write a great poem on Caligula as legislator or Hitler as anthropologist." Thus by implication our need in some sense to feel the rightness of the satirist's moral indignation is allowed. A similar sort of conclusion is reached by Elliott in his discussion of Roy Campbell's satires. Elliott is finally led to deny Campbell full satiric power because he "worked from a rotten center," because his "opinions are stupid and evil and insofar as they inform the poetry, the poetry must suffer thereby." [11]

Conversely, moral indignation focused intensely and sincerely on objects clearly deserving our reprobation scarcely insures even our attention, to say nothing of the attention of readers to come. Mr. Tuveson's comments on the relatively ineffective and timebound expressions of ideas and attitudes parallel to Swift's in

Gulliver's Travels that exist outside the artistic context of satire
or literature point up the integrity of artistic statement. Great
satire, it seems to me, cannot exist apart from a successfully
achieved sense of moral indignation that inevitably depends in
considerable degree on our sense of the rightness of the attack
on those conditions in the real world to which attention is
called. That some satire calls attention self-consciously to its wit
and art or that some satires obscure or falsify the details of the
external, historic world may complicate or even compromise
the satirist's moral position, but it is to this position as well as
to his art that we invariably return.

Aubrey Williams, in the "Introduction" to his admirable study
of *The Dunciad* (*Pope's Dunciad: A Study of its Meaning*,
London, 1953) examines the complications and misdirections to
which merely historical or moralistic approaches to *The Dunciad*
lead. His own study, he implies, will be one that "involves close
historical study but remains aesthetic criticism" and not one
which "ends up as 'sociology, biography, or other kinds of non-
aesthetic history'" (p. 3). Yet he also observes that "in any
satiric work art stands in close and peculiar relationship with
morality from the beginning. Such works appear to spring from
a blend of the artistic faculties and of the moral attitudes, either
real or assumed, within the satirist. The satirist, either in terms
of biographical reality or in terms of a fictive personality, takes
a moral position from which he lashes out at what appear to be,
in the light of his own or his assumed standards, the vices and
follies of mankind" (p. 4). The qualifications concerning the
"source" of the morality ("real or assumed," representing the
satirist's "own or his assumed standards"), derive, as a footnote
tells us, from Mack's essay "The Muse of Satire." But Mr.
Williams's concluding paragraph, for example, suggests to me
at least that these qualifications are not sharply maintained: "We
are really back at the starting point of the *Dunciad* and of this

essay—in the presence of a very real and lively war between bad writers and a poet for whom important issues were at stake. Dunces, and duncely writings, were not, to Pope, matters of little or merely personal import. Such 'words', such art, inevitably for him referred to states of mind and soul, and to the state of the social order as a whole. As Pope saw the contemporary situation, such a 'deluge of authors' (the metaphor is again worth noting) had covered England that they threatened to 'make one Mighty Dunciad of the Land'" (p. 158). Does not this language suggest that Mr. Williams finds the "vision" of *The Dunciad* ethically and not only artistically moving and significant? Moreover, is it not Pope's real self, allowing for the complications of that concept as Ehrenpreis describes them, for whom these "important issues were at stake"? I would suggest that *The Dunciad* is an important satiric work of art for us and for Mr. Williams because its ethical content artistically rendered is moving and convincing.

How moving and convincing? What is the nature of the reader's involvement with a "savage indignation" directed at issues, ideas, individuals with whom we do not necessarily have any connection? Such a question is of course ultimately related to that perennial question concerning our capacity to admire writers whose beliefs we do not share. But considering the question only as it may be related to our response to works of satire, one recalls Orwell's bemused reflections on his own response to Swift, a writer to whom he stands in opposition on nearly every intellectual issue. Yet Orwell confesses that for him the fascination of *Gulliver's Travels* "seems inexhaustible" and that if he were to list the six books to be preserved when all others were destroyed he would put *Gulliver's Travels* among them. His answer to his puzzlement is probably not fully satisfactory. Swift's power, for Orwell, is his "terrible intensity of vision" and "the durability of *Gulliver's Travels* goes to show that, if the force of belief is behind it, a world-view which only just passes the test of sanity is sufficient to produce a great work of art." [12] For most of us Swift passes the test of sanity with higher marks. But Orwell's observation about the force of Swift's belief underlines usefully the point I am making here and reminds us once again how central our sense of the satirist is in our response to the satiric work.

In discussing the satiric techniques of *A Modest Proposal* Mr. Tuveson also touches upon the question of a contemporary reader's response to Swift's attack on conditions in eighteenth-century Ireland. He suggests that Swift's method, which he describes as being "quite literally . . . a form of shock treatment," creates a work whereby "the non-seeing, the complacent or despondent acceptance of things as they are is subjected to moral trauma" and that "by extension, it has something like this effect on the modern reader; it seems to jar him into seeing anew his own world." This too is a useful suggestion because it emphasizes the interconnection between the art of satire and the sensitive reader's ethical involvement in the satirist's vision of his world.

Does one see anew his own world after reading *A Modest Proposal?* Louis I. Bredvold in an essay published some twenty years ago makes for me the most satisfying accounting of our response to the satirist's indignation. After reviewing a variety of theories about satire and acknowledging that we are left relatively defenseless if we attempt to justify the satirist's art in terms of its corrective effects in the real world, he finds that the instructive pleasure in reading great satire, the "immediate exhilaration" which we experience, "comes from the tone-restoring exercise of our sluggish moral muscles. We are summoned from our indifference and quiescence; our latent energies awake and assume definite direction and character. We participate in the communion of those men—few though they may be—for whom things matter, and with them we share the faith in the validity of universal principles." [13] To write so about satire is not to ignore the art that, in this fallen world, can produce so mysterious a result; it is to acknowledge the human and humane conditions out of which the art of satire is fashioned.

Notes

Introduction
H. JAMES JENSEN

1. See for example, John Dryden, "Preface of the Translation to the Parallel Betwixt Poetry and Painting," *Works*, eds. Scott-Saintsbury, vol. 17 (Edinburgh, 1882–93), p. 295.

In Satire's Falling City
EARL MINER

1. See Leo Strauss, *The City and Man* (Chicago, 1964), and Maynard Mack, *The Garden and the City* (Toronto, 1969).

2. I refer of course to Hobbes's *Answer* to Davenant: see *Critical Essays of the Seventeenth Century*, ed. Joel E. Spingarn, 3 vols. (Bloomington, Ind., 1957), 2: 54–5. A seemingly little known expression of the symbolic import of the city is Herrick's poem, "His Returne to London," which I have sometimes thought the first "Augustan" poem in English.

3. My copy, "decima editio," *Quinti Horatii Flacci Opera*, is a London reprint of 1790; see p. 389, line 1, note. See also *Epodes*, vii, and the ironic close to *Epodes*, ii. In Horace, the contrast is between "magna . . . Roma" and "hospitio modico." A similar usage by Cicero, *De Senectute*, 23. 84, shows that the Stoic sense of the "inn"

for life probably functions in Horace as well. In the lines following in Horace's satire, the usual crowded satiric scene plainly emerges.

4. See O. B. Hardison, *The Enduring Monument* (Chapel Hill, N.C., 1962); Ovid, *Metamorphoses*, XV, 234–6 for the locus classicus on the ravages of time and age, and XV, 871–9 for the triumph of immortal art over such forces.

5. *Aeneid*, I, 437: "o fortunati, quorum iam moenia surgunt!"

6. Those writers most applicable to a discussion primarily based on verse satire are: Mary Claire Randolph, "The Formal Verse Satire," *PQ*, 21 (1942), 368–84, and "The Medical Concept in English Satiric Theory," *SP*, 38 (1941), 125–57; Maynard Mack, "The Muse of Satire," *Yale Review*, 41 (1951–52), 80–92; Robert C. Elliott, *The Power of Satire* (Princeton, 1960); Alvin B. Kernan, *The Cankered Muse* (New Haven, 1959) and *The Plot of Satire* (New Haven, 1965); Ronald Paulson, *The Fictions of Satire* (Baltimore, 1967). Perhaps the work bearing most nearly on this essay is, however, Michael A. Seidel's dissertation, "Satiric Theory and the Degeneration of the State: The Tyrant and Mob in Satiric Literature of the Restoration and Early Eighteenth Century" (UCLA, 1970). Many more works might be cited, and especially analyses of individual poems. Northrop Frye's comments on comedy in *Anatomy of Criticism* (Princeton, 1957) are more useful for understanding the fundamental principles of satire than are his comments on satire.

7. See "A Discourse Concerning the Original and Progress of Satire" in *Of Dramatic Poesy and Other Critical Essays*, ed. George Watson, 2 vols. (London and New York, 1962), 2: 71–155; hereafter this collection is cited as Watson. His notes specify Dryden's sources, although, following Ker, he is mistaken about the "De Satyra" of Daniel Heinsius, which Dryden had read in the much-expanded 1629 edition of Horace. See Paul Sellin, *Daniel Heinsius and Stuart England* (Leiden and London, 1968), p. 179. *The Works of John Dryden*, vol. 4 (ed. William Frost et al.) will treat such matters in detail.

8. I am at work on a discussion that will, I hope, draw out the implications of this premise, or assertion.

9. The announcement of *Potatoes* is taken from *The Book Exchange,* published by Fudge & Co., Ltd., London; Cat. no. 254 (May 1969), p. 14.

10. *The Scriblerian,* 1 (1969), 34.

11. Quoted from the fine study by Ruth Nevo, *The Dial of Virtue* (Princeton, 1963), p. 210.

12. George Puttenham, *The Arte of English Poesie* (London, 1589), 3: xviii. "Dry *Bobs*" substitutes for "the Drie Mock," *Ironia.* The rest are: *Antiphrasis, Sarcasmus, Micterismus, Charientismus.*

13. Watson, 2: 145.

14. Watson, 2: 145. Having correctly discussed satire as a conception derived from *satura lanx,* "abundant platter," and going on to concern with the mixed Varonnian satire, Dryden must cut his argument very fine (2: 145–6) to demand unity.

15. Watson, 2: 146.

16. Watson, 2: 146, 147.

17. Watson, 2: 149.

18. *To Sir Godfrey Kneller,* l. 94. I have a discussion of the "context" of that line and of the poem in my compilation, *Seventeenth-Century Imagery* (Berkeley and Los Angeles, 1971), under the title, "Dryden's Eikon Basilike: *To Sir Godfrey Kneller.*"

19. See H. T. Swedenberg, "Dryden's Obsessive Concern with the Heroic," *SP,* Extra Series, No. 4 (January 1967), p. 26.

20. It goes almost without saying that Dryden's relation of epic and satire may have been influenced by prosodic considerations: in Latin the dactylic hexameter and in English the iambic pentameter, especially in couplets, served for both genres. Variation led to other genres, as Ovid wittily showed in *Amores,* I, i.

21. Watson, 1: 101.

22. Similarly, the discussion of wit and imagination in the same "Account" (1: 97–9) seems to me crucial on those matters.

23. *"To* P. Rupert," *The Poems of John Cleveland,* ed. Brian Morris and Eleanor Withington (Oxford, 1967), p. 33, l. 26.

24. Cf. *Gondibert,* II, v, 36:4.

25. See A. R. Heiserman, "Satire in the *Utopia," PMLA,* 78 (1963), 163–74; and Robert C. Elliott, "The Shape of Utopia," *ELH,* 30 (1963), 317–34.

26. Watson, 2: 193.

27. Watson, 2: 202.

28. Such matters as these provided the basis of a more theoretical and comparative discussion in a paper given before the colloquium of the Center for Japanese and Korean Studies, University of California, Berkeley, February 19, 1970: "Literary Bounds and Transformations: Japanese and Western Evidence Compared."

29. Frye, *Anatomy of Criticism,* pp. 43, 163.

30. For the concept of degeneration as the modal feature of satire, I am indebted to Michael A. Seidel (see n. 6, above). Because I was his dissertation adviser, we have been able to talk through our ideas prior to the publication of his work and this paper. I am grateful

for that and for the comments by him, by Robert C. Elliott, and Murray Krieger on this paper.

31. See Mary Claire Randolph on "The Medical Image," n. 6, above; and Bernard Schilling, *Dryden and the Conservative Myth* (New Haven, 1961), especially pp. 240–54. As so often, Butler brings things together in a harsh focus, combining satire's moral function, magic, politics, disease, and medicine: "Morall Representations . . . like Charmes easily Cure those Fantastique Distempers in Governments, which being neglected grow too stubborn to obey any but . . . Rigid Medecines" (*Characters and Passages from Note-books*, ed. A. R. Waller [Cambridge, England, 1908], pp. 431–2).

32. *Gulliver's Travels* etc., ed. William Alfred Eddy (Oxford, 1933), pp. 141–2.

33. Watson, 2: 130.

34. Krieger, "The 'Frail China Jar' . . . ," *Centennial Review of the Arts and Sciences*, 5 (1961), 176–94; reprinted in Maynard Mack, ed., *Essential Articles for the Study of Alexander Pope*, rev. ed. (Hamden, Conn., 1968), pp. 301–19.

35. Scaliger, . . . *Poetices Libri Septem* (Lyons, 1561), p. 337: "ita Epistolae proponunt ea quibus a vitio abistineamus: Satyra illis pugnat quibus vitia extirpentur." Pope's understanding of the matters treated in this paragraph is evident from *The Second Satire of Doctor Donne*. Donne had written (17–18): "One would move Love by rithmes; but witchcrafts charms / Bring not now their old feares, nor their old harmes." Which Pope altered to read: "One sings the Fair, but Songs no longer move, / No Rat is rhym'd to death, nor Maid to love" (21–22).

36. Watson, 2: 137.

37. These remarkable verses were printed for the first time by George deF. Lord, ed., *Poems on Affairs of State*, vol. 1 (New Haven, 1963), p. liii.

38. *To My Honour'd Kinsman,* ll. 207–9. See also *Eleonora,* ll. 375–7. The best study I know of a single group of seventeenth-century panegyrics is that by Barbara K. Lewalski, "Donne's Poetry of Compliment," in *Seventeenth-Century Imagery* (see n. 18, above).

39. *Lives of the English Poets,* ed. G. Birkbeck Hill, 3 vols. (Oxford, 1935), 2: 244.

40. Hill, 3: 191.

41. Congreve in *The Dramatick Works of John Dryden, Esq.,* 6 vols. (London, 1717), 1, Dedication, sig. a6^r.

42. *An Essay on Man,* 4: 168. Quotations of Pope have been taken from the relevant volumes in the Twickenham edition; of Dryden's poetry from *The Poems and Fables of John Dryden,* ed. James Kinsley, 4 vols. (Oxford, 1958); of Milton from *John Milton Complete Poems and Major Prose,* ed. Merritt Y. Hughes (New York, 1957).

Pope's Illusive Temple of Infamy
MICHAEL ROSENBLUM

1. W. B. Carnochan's *Lemuel Gulliver's Mirror for Man* (Berkeley, 1968) has presented Swift as the self-conscious satirist. According to Carnochan *Gulliver's Travels* is "of all satires, the most self-aware. It illustrates a paradox that has for better or worse established itself in the modern mind: that great art is typically, perhaps even necessarily, its own subject, is about itself" (p. 13). The necessary self-consciousness of the satirist is one of the implications of Robert C. Elliott's *The Power of Satire: Magic, Ritual, Art* (Princeton, 1960).

2. Kenneth Burke, *Attitudes Towards History* (Boston, 1961), pp. 49–50.

3. "The First Satire of the Second Book of Horace Imitated," *The Poems of Alexander Pope,* ed. John Butt (New Haven, 1966), p. 614, l. 14. I have used this edition, a one-volume edition of the Twickenham text, for all Pope's poetry other than *The Dunciad.*

4. Maynard Mack, *The Garden and the City* (Toronto, 1969), p. 193.

5. *The Dunciad,* ed. James Sutherland (New Haven, 1953), p. 107. I have used this edition (the Twickenham) for all references to *The Dunciad.* "A" or "B" indicates references to the A (1729) or B (1743) texts in this edition.

6. Sheldon Sacks, *Fiction and the Shape of Belief* (Berkeley, 1967), p. 26, and Ronald Paulson, *The Fictions of Satire* (Baltimore, 1967), p. 3. Edward Rosenheim in *Swift and the Satirist's Art* (Chicago, 1958) argues that "satire cannot be fully effective if we fail to understand what the satirist genuinely believes and wishes us to believe about the issues reflected in his work. When we identify his victim, we establish the 'true' direction of his assault, locating his final target in the realm of actuality. Fiction serves a satiric purpose only when we are aware of the manner and extent of its departure from authentic fact and belief" (pp. 179–80). Although Sacks, Paulson, and Rosenheim do not have the same view of satire, I do not think I misrepresent their positions in saying that they share a broadly rhetorical view of satire. An exception to the prevailing rhetorical view is John Clark's *Form and Frenzy in Swift's "Tale of a Tub"* (Ithaca, 1970), a work which I saw only after writing this paper.

7. Northrop Frye, *The Anatomy of Criticism* (Princeton, 1957), p. 245.

8. Paulson, p. 152.

9. Hugh Kenner, *The Counterfeiters* (Bloomington, Ind., 1968), p. 30.

10. Edward Said, "Swift's Tory Anarchy," *Eighteenth Century Studies*, 3 (Fall 1969), pp. 51, 54.

11. Austin Warren, "Pope," *Essential Articles for the Study of Alexander Pope*, ed. Maynard Mack (Hamden, 1968), p. 87.

12. Paulson, p. 5.

13. T. S. Eliot, *Essays on Elizabethan Drama* (New York, 1956), p. 80.

14. M. H. Abrams, *The Mirror and the Lamp* (New York, 1958), p. 6.

15. *The Correspondence of Alexander Pope*, ed. George Sherburn (Oxford, 1956), 2:468.

16. Sutherland, p. 411.

17. Pope writes to Caryll on April 8, 1729 about *The Dunciad*: "The other book is written (all but the poem) by two or three of my friends, and a droll book it is" (3:31). On May 30, 1729 he says: "My friends who took so much pains to comment upon it, must come off with the public as they can" (3:36). And again, more emphatically: "As to the Notes, I am weary of telling a great Truth, which is, that I am not Author of 'em" (3:165). Despite Pope's insistence on this "great truth" his modern editor remains unconvinced: "There seems to be no escaping the conclusion, therefore, that when Pope decided to publish the *Dunciad* with Notes Variorum it was he himself (with Savage acting, perhaps, as a sort of secretary) who worked through his four volumes of Libels, Jacob's *Poetical Register,* Winstanley's *Lives of the Poets,* and other works of reference or abuse" (Sutherland, xxvii).

18. "Beyond lending his name to it, Cleland had probably not much more to do with writing the Letter than Mrs. Anne Dodd had with publishing it" (Sutherland, xxv).

19. "Do you care I shou'd say any thing farther how much that poem is yours? Since certainly without you it had never been. Would to God we were together for the rest of our lives! The whole weight of Scriblers would just serve to find us amusement, and not more" (Pope to Swift, 2:522). Sherburn is skeptical: "Pope is somewhat too eager to involve Swift with himself as an ally against the Dunces."

20. I am relying on two of Sutherland's conjectures here. The first, that Pope intended the publication of *Peri Bathous* as "a sort of ground bait for the subsequent sport of the *Dunciad*" (xvi), seems to have won fairly wide acceptance. The second is more speculative but still plausible: that Pope "arranged that a spurious proof sheet of the revised *Dunciad* should be 'stolen' from the printer's and sent to [Cibber]," to provoke Cibber into writing something like *A Letter from Mr. Cibber to Mr. Pope* (Sutherland, xxxiv).

21. The terms are Geoffrey Hartman's in "Toward Literary History," *Daedalus* (Spring 1970), 356.

22. Mack has demonstrated the increasingly political nature of the references in Pope's revisions: "Small changes in successive texts of the three book *Dunciad* had already for some years been deepening its political complexion" (p. 150). "In general, then, both by added notes and added or revised lines, Pope made the political intent of the *New Dunciad* of 1742 yet more explicit in Book IV of 1743 which it became. At the same time, to the Variorum *Dunciad* of 1729, which provided Books I–III, he added a vein of political innuendo that was not originally present" (p. 155).

23. Aubrey Williams, *Pope's Dunciad* (Baton Rouge, 1955), p. 62. A good deal of what I have to say in this essay is a restatement in different terms of the argument of William's third chapter, "The Variorum Dunciad."

24. "In the meantime his *Dulness* grows and flourishes as if he was there already. It will indeed be a noble work: the many will stare

at it, the few will smile, and all his Patrons from Bickerstaffe to Gulliver will rejoice, to see themselves adorn'd in that immortal piece" (Bolingbrooke and Pope to Swift, February 1727/8, 2:472).

25. The line is "True to the bottom, see Concanen creep" (A II, p. 137, l. 287). Pope is probably responding to Concanen's assertion that another line in which Pope had used asterisks referred to the King and Queen. The line is A II, 287: "Thy dragons Magistrates and Peers shall taste." Pope's note to the line reads: "It stood in the first edition with blanks, *Thy dragons *** and ***. Concanen* was sure, 'they must needs mean no-body but the *King* and *Queen,* and said he would insist it was so, till the Poet clear'd himself by filling up the blanks otherwise agreeably to the context, and consistent with his *allegiance*' " (p. 184).

26. "By transferring the same ridicule from one to another, he destroyed its efficacy; for, by shewing that what he had said of one was ready to say of another, he reduced himself to the insignificance of his own magpye, who from his cage calls cuckold at a venture" (*Lives of the Poets* [London, 1959], 2:288).

27. Horace Gregory, trans., *The Metamorphoses* (New York, 1960), pp. 300–301.

28. Mack in his concluding sentence makes the figure of Prospero the final emblem for Pope's relation to his subjects: "Under his magisterial wand, like the wrecked voyagers in *The Tempest,* lords and rich men, ministers and society-wenches, kings, courtiers, Quakers, clowns, and good Ralph Allens move through the paces of an intricate satirical ballet, which combines the features of reality and dream" (p. 236).

29. The poem has been read by critics as expressing either the wish (to control dullness) or the fear (that it can't be contained). Thus, Alvin Kernan in *The Plot of Satire* (New Haven, 1965) has argued that Pope "has so arranged his poem that this ultimate expansion is

at once a contraction. At the very moment that dullness becomes everything, everything becomes nothing, for dullness is finally nothingness, vacuity, matter without form or idea" (p. 115). On the other hand Thomas Edwards, Jr. glosses these lines (B IV 5–8) in this way: "The critical intelligence that made the poem possible must bow before the irresistible onslaught of *nature*—a nature no longer seen as a synonym for light and order but as a label for a ceaseless mutability destroying all that makes life dignified or even possible" ("Light and Nature: A Reading of the Dunciad" in Mack, *Essential Articles,* p. 785).

30. Elliott has suggested the negative tendencies of "major satire": "Let the conscious intent of the artist be what it will, the local attack cannot be contained: the ironic language eats its way in implication through the most powerful-seeming structures" (*Power of Satire,* p. 274). "The pressure of his [Swift's] art works directly against the ostensibly conservative function which it appears to serve. Instead of shoring up foundations, it tears them down. It is revolutionary" (pp. 274–5).

Swift: The View from within the Satire

ERNEST TUVESON

1. Dryden, "Preface to *An Evening's Love,*" in *Of Dramatic Poesy and Other Critical Works,* ed. G. Watson (Everyman's Library, 1962), 1:149.

2. Thomas Blount, *Glossographia* (1656).

3. John Bulloker, *English Expositour* (1616).

4. *The Gentleman Instructed in the Conduct of a Virtuous and Happy Life,* 9th ed. (1727), p. 9.

5. The quotations from Swift are from *Gulliver's Travels and Other Writings,* ed. Landa (Boston, 1960).

6. Edward Rosenheim, *Swift and the Satirist's Art* (Chicago, 1963), p. 44.

7. Mark Schorer, "Afterword" to *Main Street* (New American Library, 1961).

8. William Dampier, *A New Voyage Around the World,* ed. Sir Albert Gray (New York, 1908), p. 312. It is tempting to speculate as to whether Swift himself could have known more about the "correction" of Dampier's narrative than we know. Dampier did have his work "revised and corrected by friends": Dampier was a kind of lion while he was writing the work; in the 1690's, on one occasion he dined with Pepys and Evelyn, and he was patronized by such notables as the Earl of Halifax.

9. John Wesley, *Works* (New York, 1827), 9:167. The statement is dated 1756.

10. Wesley, 9:313.

11. Wesley, 5:193. This is from a sermon, dating, apparently, between 1737 and 1747.

12. Boileau-Despreaux, *Oeuvres* (Dresden, 1767), 1:10.

13. Ian Watt, "The Ironic Function of Augustan Prose," in James Sutherland and Ian Watt, *Restoration and Augustan Prose* (William Andrews Clark Library, 1956), p. 35.

Afterword
MALVIN R. ZIRKER, JR.

1. Alvin Kernan, *The Cankered Muse* (New Haven, 1959), and *The Plot of Satire* (New Haven, 1965); and Ronald Paulson, *The Fictions of Satire* (Baltimore, 1967) and *Satire and the Novel in*

Eighteenth-Century England (New Haven, 1967). See also Edward Rosenheim's *Swift and the Satirist's Art* (Chicago, 1963); Sheldon Sack's *Fiction and the Shape of Belief* (Berkeley, 1964), primarily chapter 1; and Northrop Frye's *Anatomy of Criticism* (Princeton, 1957), primarily pp. 223–39 and 309–14.

2. "*L'amour-propre* des satiriques est très développé: ils sont *vaniteux, ambitieux,* avides de gloire, orgueilleux et *altiers* parfois à un degré frisant la pathologie," p. 21.

3. *The Yale Review,* 41 (1951), 80–92.

4. Kernan, *The Cankered Muse,* p. 22.

5. Bronson, *In Search of Chaucer* (Toronto, 1960), pp. 25–6.

6. Bronson, pp. 29–30.

7. Irvin Ehrenpreis, "Personae," in *Restoration and Eighteenth-Century Literature: Essays in Honor of Alan Dugald McKillop,* ed. Carroll Camden (Chicago, 1963), pp. 25–37.

8. Ehrenpreis, pp. 30–31.

9. Ehrenpreis, p. 32.

10. Ehrenpreis, p. 37.

11. Robert C. Elliott, *The Power of Satire* (Princeton, 1960), p. 240.

12. George Orwell, "Politics vs. Literature: An Examination of *Gulliver's Travels,*" as printed in *Discussions of Jonathan Swift,* ed. John Traugott (Boston, 1962), p. 91.

13. Louis I. Bredvold, "A Note in Defence of Satire," in *Studies in the Literature of the Augustan Age,* ed. Richard C. Boys (Michigan, 1952), p. 13.

3 5282 00132 5920